The Tactical Marketing Handbook

91 Ways to Get More Engagement, More Sales, and More Profit

Kit Sadgrove

WHO THIS BOOK IS FOR

If you're in marketing or sales, or you have something to promote, this book is for you. It's the first and only comprehensive guide to tactical marketing.

Do you wrestle with tasks like these:

- Launch a new product
- Improve your website
- Reach more prospects
- Get repeat business
- Create a sales promotion
- Get more revenue
- Beat off the competition
- Increase your profit margin

If you're tackling any of these challenges, I've written the book for you.

You might be working on the client side, or in an agency. You could be a consultant, a coach, or just learning about marketing. Either way, you'll find good ideas in here.

WHAT YOU'LL LEARN

The Tactical Marketing Handbook is a practical source of actionable ideas. You won't need all of them - but there *will* be many nuggets you can use. Here's what it covers:

- 14 ways to create new products

- 10 ideas for planning your marketing

- 6 methods for beating the competition

- 7 things you should do to enhance your product or service

- 12 ways to increase your price and boost your revenue

- 7 tactics to make your customers happy

- 13 communication tactics

- 20 ideas for promoting your products

- 5 ways to run a Sale

- 17 "must-have" actions to enhance your online effectiveness

You'll find the book focuses on actions that will make a difference, whether that's greater awareness, a stronger brand identity, or just more revenue. In short, if it isn't actionable, it's not in this book.

WHY LISTEN TO ME?

Hello, I'm Kit Sadgrove. I'm a long-time marketer and the author of several business books, including "Copywriting Frameworks, Formulas and Checklists".

I've worked for a major management consultancy, and been employed in two top 10-advertising agencies.

Each year my consultancy practice at Ixant.com helps a limited number of clients to achieve a marketing breakthrough, using our 9 Levers™ framework. If you think I might be able to assist you, just get in touch.

CONTENTS

Tactics means doing what you can, with what you have.
- Saul Alinsky

1. WHY TACTICS CAN WORK BETTER THAN STRATEGY

I have a confession. I'm not a fan of marketing strategy. I say its value is over-stated.

Why? Because most businesses can't readily change their underlying strategy. Let's take some examples.

1. **You're a manufacturer.** You sell a range of pumps, to all the people that need pumps. They include construction firms, boat builders, labs and car companies. You'd like more sales. And so, what are your options?

You could create products that are slightly similar to pumps, such as vacuums, but your main business doesn't give you much room for big changes. You're limited to tactics.

2. **You're a software business**. You sell backup storage, a bit like Dropbox or OneDrive. Your main costs are your servers, a bit of tech support and some software development. Can you change your over-arching strategy? Not really. But you *can* amend your pricing, brand image and promotion. It's tactics, again.

3. **You're a bricks and mortar fashion retailer,** with an ecommerce operation. And you'd like more profit. What are your options? You could close your shops and become online-

only. That's a nuclear option. Apart from that, the main things you can change are: the number of shops, the layout of your shops, your stock, and the look of your website. Apart from that nuclear option, you're limited to tactics.

My point is: most businesses have limited options for change. It's rare to see a business that has made a dramatic change in its strategy.

A handful of companies have succeeded. Netflix went from distributing other people's content to being a film producer. IT companies like Microsoft and Cisco changed to a subscription model. And Dutch electronics giant Philips moved from lightbulbs to healthcare diagnostics. But they're few in number. And they require more insight, courage and talent than most of us possess.

There are a few examples of *new entrants* overturning a market, such as Uber and Airbnb. But that's about creating a new market from scratch, and it's vanishingly rare. This book focuses on the majority of businesses that are dealing with day-to-day issues.

In the three examples above, you may have spotted some opportunities for growth. The software business can do more marketing. The fashion retailer can change its stock. The pump company can investigate similar products, such as vacuums.

And each of these actions could lead to new customers and more revenue. It's a practical approach that produces results.

MARKETING STRATEGY TENDS TO BE ABSTRACT

You may have seen the 'business model canvas' diagrams that set out your choices. Customer segments. Value propositions. Cost structure. I can see your eyes glazing over.

At that level, beloved by academics, it's hard to find actionable change. As Winston Churchill said: "However beautiful the strategy, you should occasionally look at the results."

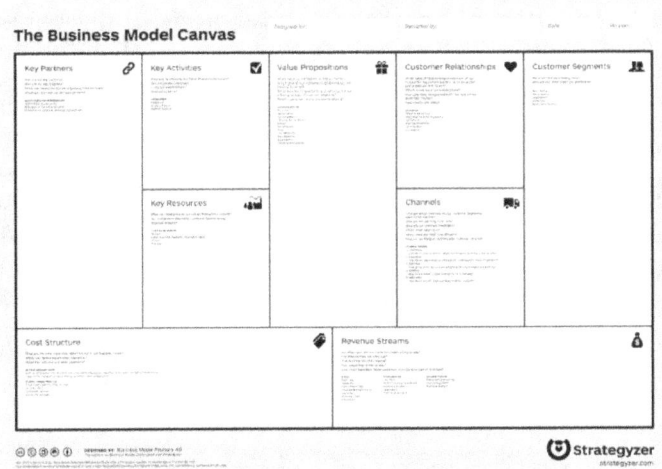

Business Model Canvas. Source: Wikipedia

And the business model canvas is mostly suited to new startups, not existing businesses.

But this apparently negative talk doesn't mean you can't make change. You can achieve much through tactical marketing.

THE ADVANTAGES OF TACTICS

Tactical marketing is a more hands-on approach to marketing. It focuses on specific actions to achieve specific goals. It's action-oriented. And it works, because it helps you implement your goals, and measure the effectiveness of your marketing efforts. You work with the cards you've been dealt.

Strategic marketing is about long-term planning and the overall direction of the business. It's a more theoretical approach, as it focuses on the company's overall objectives. So, while strategic marketing is essential for the long-term, you need tactical marketing to achieve those goals right now.

Tactical marketing is also more adaptable and flexible than strategic marketing. It allows marketers to quickly adapt to changes in the market and to take advantage of new opportunities. In contrast, strategic marketing can be slow to develop, and may not be as responsive to changes in the market. How well does anyone's five-year plan stand up to scrutiny?

In addition, tactical marketing allows you to target specific customers, and thus can be more cost-effective. By focusing on specific tactics, you can reach your target audience more effectively, and with a smaller budget. This can be particularly beneficial for small businesses that may not have the resources for a large, strategic marketing campaign.

TACTICAL MARKETING ENCOURAGES ACTION

It's really easy to say, "We're going to add a new flavour". People know what that means and how to do it. It's where the rubber meets the road.

But if you say "We're going to workshop a review program to investigate our customer strategy," well, that's hard to grasp. And little good will come of it.

Too many marketing books are bland. Their solutions are vague and hard to implement. They tend to cover the same old ground. Segmentation. Positioning. The theory of product development. They're great for students, but they're not actionable. They have limited practicality.

And the same applies to "marketing strategy". Take the SWOT analysis, the well-known acronym that asks you to identify your strengths, weaknesses, opportunities and threats. You do the analysis. And then what? What's the outcome? What are you supposed to do with the analysis? Let's take a hypothetical SWOT:

Strengths: You have good products, and you're well-known to your customers.

Weaknesses: Your sales aren't growing.

Opportunities: You could find new markets for your products.

Threats: You have dangerous competitors.

It's vague, isn't it? It's not actionable. And that's the problem with much of today's "marketing strategy".

Change doesn't take place from a strategy session.

It happens when someone says, "How about we do X?"

It's usually an impromptu thing that occurs when someone muses, "What could we do that's different?" Or "How do we increase sales?" It's the simple questions and idle thoughts that make a difference.

Some marketers deprecate the word 'Tactics'. Maybe it sounds cheap and small-minded? It's not as glamorous as "Strategy". But we shouldn't let pride stand in the way of change. If tactics work, let's use them.

When I worked for a management consultancy, I was occasionally accused of 'marketing opportunism'. Some of my colleagues thought it lacked gravity. A few years later, after I'd left, the business ceased trading, having failed to move with the times. It gives me no pleasure to say that, because it had been a solid business with good people.

THE ISTO FRAMEWORK

ISTO shows how you can use all the tools at your disposal to create change.

We start with **Intention**, which is what you're aiming to

achieve.

Next comes **Strategy** and **Tactics.** These are the tools you will use. I've deliberately put them on the same canvas, because it is hard to decide where strategy ends and tactics begins.

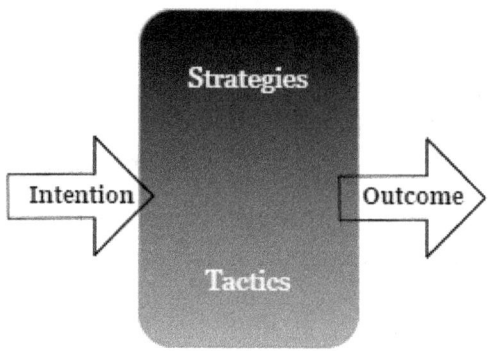

Big impact. But...
Difficult. Expensive. High risk.

Low impact. But....
Easy. Inexpensive. Low risk.

The ISTO Principle

And frankly, the precise definitions don't matter. That's why I created ISTO. It's to demonstrate that *whatever works is the one you should use.*

The only thing that matters is to use the tool that achieves the **Outcome** you want.

A builder will rummage around in their tool box until they find the tool that will do the job. If it doesn't work, they'll drop it back into the box and use something else. The same applies to marketing - as long as you've identified your intention and the expected outcome.

In this book, some tools are large scale, while others are a matter of detail. And that's because each one has its use. One day, you'll be thinking about how to earn more customer loyalty, and the next you'll be planning a trade show.

To emphasize that the book is practical, I've added a 'How to' at the end of most topics. You can use it to convert words into action. The exceptions are where I've already included the detailed "how to" in the text.

But there are some risks in focusing solely on tactics

Tactics aren't a cure-all. Small-scale tactics will win you short-term sales, but won't save you if you're in the wrong market, with the wrong products or pricing, and doing inadequate promotion.

Later in this book, I talk about Jim Collins' book, "Good to Great", and his Doom Loop. He says management often responds to declining sales in the wrong way. They fire the CEO, acquire other businesses or run sales promotions.

But the activities he mentions are not really about tactics – they're a failure to identify the problem. And maybe firing the CEO or doing an acquisition could be the right course of action?

So, use tactics appropriately, where they're needed. Treat this book as a source of ideas.

Now let's get started. We begin with innovation.

The riskiest thing we can do
is just maintain the status quo.
- Bob Iger

2. INNOVATION TACTICS

ADD NEW PRODUCTS SUCCESSFULLY

Like people, products grow old. Newer products come along, as technology and fashion change. And while you can update your existing products, there's a risk that your design or niche is in decline. Hence, you need to constantly search for new products and markets.

Creating new products lets you stay relevant, grow your market share, and remain competitive in today's changing business environment.

Stay aware. You should continually evaluate your current product line and consider how you can innovate and improve your offerings to meet the evolving needs of your customers.

Market research. You can conduct surveys, focus groups, and analyze customer data to understand what consumers are looking for in a product. But be aware that respondents can't tell you whether a hypothetical product will succeed.

Partnerships: You can also create new products through partnerships and collaborations with other companies or organizations. Tesla is known for its electric vehicles, but it also has partnerships with solar panel manufacturers to offer a complete renewable energy solution for its customers. By working with other companies, you can combine your resources and expertise to create new products that meet the needs of customers in unique and innovative ways.

Internal development. Finally, you can create new products through internal research and development efforts. By investing in your own R&D department, you can develop new products that you believe will be in demand in the future. Pharmaceutical companies invest heavily in R&D to discover and develop new drugs to treat various diseases.

How to create new products

1. Find ideas. Achieve this by being alert to new things, and by benchmarking your competitors and comparators.

2. Assess the size and fit of each opportunity. Is it big enough? How much time and cost will be involved?

3. Through research, test its viability, and modify its functionality.

4. Launch the product.

5. Modify it in response to feedback.

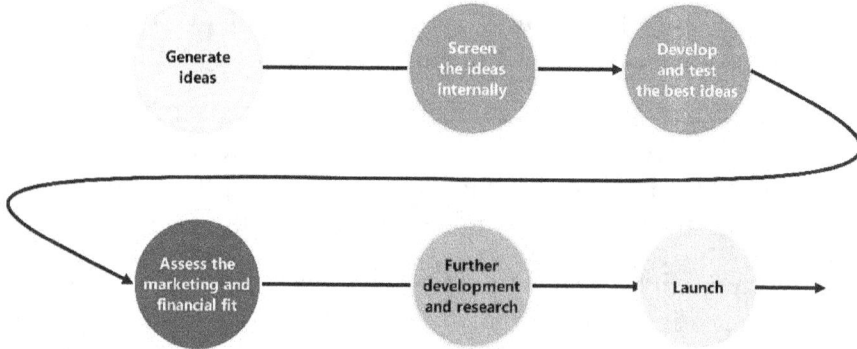

New product development plan

The MVP

Popularized by Eric Ries, the Minimum Viable Product (MVP) is a way to launch new products fast.

In summary, you create a product with just enough features to attract early adopters. That lets you:

- see how many people buy the product

- review get their feedback, which permits subsequent development

- assess whether people continue to use the product.

It's useful for startups that would want to get to market quickly. But it also stops established businesses from spending too much time and money on products that subsequently fail.

So many things get in the way of a product launch. Perfectionism, indecision, too many options, and the fear of failure. All these act as a brake. The MVP cuts through that. It's a build-measure-learn feedback loop.

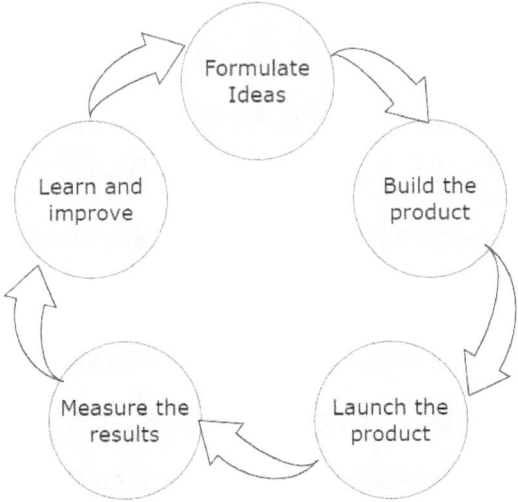

MVP Model

But there are risks. You can create a product with irritating bugs, a complex user interface, or insufficient functions. If so, consumers will turn away from it. And normally, you only get one chance. People make up their minds quickly. So, an insufficiently thought-out MVP can ruin the future of a perfectly good product.

FIND A PARTNER

Most businesses go it alone, learning as they go. Partnership isn't for them; they fear the loss of control, the sharing of trade secrets, and the complexities of dealing with other businesses.

But in doing so, they can miss out on some opportunities. No one business can know everything about their products, technologies and markets.

Partnering with individuals or other companies can bring a range of benefits, including access to new markets, complementary resources, shared knowledge and expertise, and increased innovation.

Swedish fast fashion retailer H&M teamed up with Alexander Wang, the American fashion designer, previously creative director for Balenciaga. The outcome was limited period branded clothing ranges. The two companies don't share the same audience, so H&M benefited from a high-end fashion look, while Wang gained revenue and exposure to a wider audience.

Partnerships are more complicated than simple supplier/customer relationships, and more time-consuming; so both parties have to be committed to the deal. Both teams have to work well on a personal level, need to be aware of cultural differences, and have a way of dealing with conflict. So it isn't something you want to rush into.

How to find a partner

1. Define your weaknesses, such as lack of expertise in technology, packaging or design.

2. Alternatively, consider what markets you might like to reach but lack the resources.

3. Draw up a short list of businesses, colleges or experts who might be suitable for a partnership.

4. Identify what benefits such a relationship would bring to the other party.

5. Enter into discussions with a suitable partner.

6. Seal the relationship with a contract. It may need to specify the duration of the relationship, an agreement that each party will not ally with others in the industry, and that commercial secrets will remain confidential.

VERTICAL DIVERSIFICATION

Looking for growth? Why not expand up or down your supply chain? Let's say you sell niche foods to consumers. Going up the chain will mean moving into the wholesale or bulk goods area. Higher still involves becoming an importer or grower.

Going downstream involves getting closer to your customers, rather than relying on retailers. So, you might set up your own shops. A brewer might set up a stall at fairs or festivals.

Diversifying vertically is a relatively safe bet because, though your involvement in the market, you'll be familiar with how your suppliers or customers operate. And buying an existing business with an established track record reduces the risk still further.

This type of diversification brings several benefits, including:

- **More revenue**: By having more sections of the market, you earn more income.

- **Additional customer segments**. Going up or down the line brings the possibility of customers that were previously denied to you.

- **Improved efficiency**: Integrating new operations into the existing supply chain and distribution network can increase your efficiency and reduce your costs. That in turn can make you more competitive.

- **More control**. You're less reliant on third parties for the supply or delivery of your products. It reduces the risk of unexpected price increases or even being de-listed by a retailer.

But vertical diversification also comes with some risks, including:

- **Resource constraints**: Expanding into new operations can require significant investment in terms of time, money, and other resources. This can put a strain on your finances and divert attention from your core operations.

- **Complexity**: Integrating new operations into your existing business can be complex and requires careful planning and execution. If not managed properly, it can lead to operational difficulties and negatively affect your company's performance.

- **Alienation**: Moving upstream may cause alarm among your competitors, who will see the move as a way to control them or even squeeze them out. This can disrupt the good relations that have been built up. Companies that were hitherto contented to supplier you may decide not to no longer stock your products.

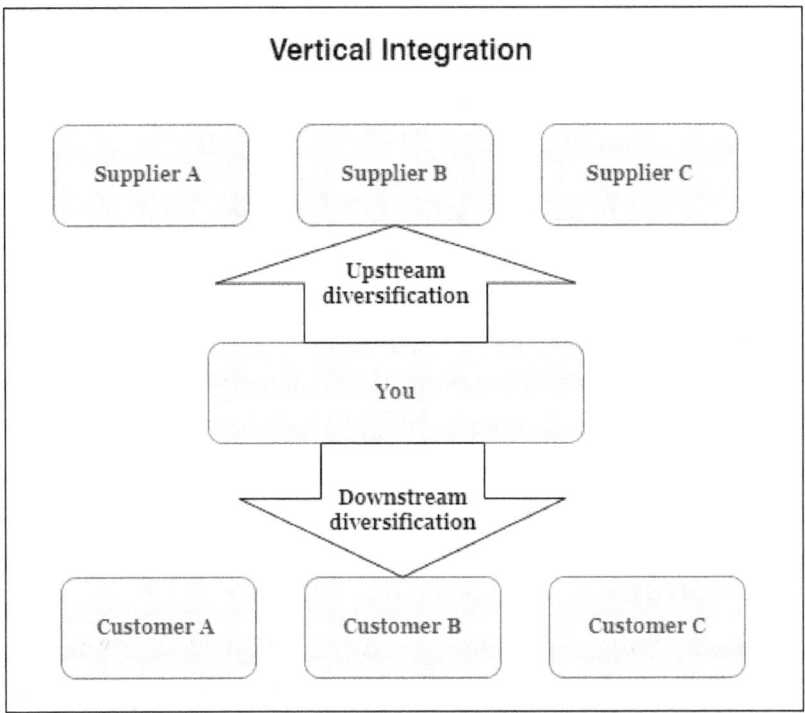

Upstream and downstream vertical integration

IMPROVE YOUR EXISTING PRODUCTS

Updating existing products is the poor relation of that handsome, charming newcomer, new product development. Who wants to tinker with something that most people say works perfectly fine?

Yet, improving existing products is crucial for maintaining your market share, staying competitive, and meeting the evolving needs and preferences of your customers. It lets you increase customer satisfaction and loyalty, and differentiate your business from your competitors. So, how do you achieve that?

Understand the goal. Continuous improvement, once limited to the shop floor, should be a marketing aim as well. That means allocating time and structures to ensure it happens.

Customer feedback. You gather customer feedback to understand what improvements customers would like to see in the product. This feedback can come from surveys, social media, and other customer interactions. By taking into account customer preferences, you can make product changes that better meet their needs.

Competitor review. Read reviews of competitors' products. Identify strong and weak points and missing features.

Stay current. You should keep up with advances in technology and industry trends to ensure your products are using the latest and most efficient techniques and features. This can involve incorporating new features such as improved security, more user-friendly interfaces, and enhanced performance.

Research. Software businesses can ask loyal customers to test a beta version of their product, while many authors ask fans to read a book before it goes to press. Retailers can test a new look in a limited number of stores, and manufacturers can produce limited editions to assess consumer demand.

Cost and prioritize. You have to prioritize which improvements are essential and which can wait. Making too many changes at once can be overwhelming for customers, and you should focus on making incremental improvements that will add the most value.

Be aware of the risks. And the risk of improving your product is that customers may hate it. 'New Coke' almost sank Coca-Cola, no matter how much better it might have been. And whenever you decide (or are forced) to upgrade a product, you'll find essential or beloved features have been moved or deleted.

People get used to your product, and if you then fiddle with it, they can get confused and irritated. There's also a risk that you can make the product worse, produce unexpected problems, or add features that make the product harder to use. You have to weigh up how much reliance to place on customer grumbles, and identify real issues before doing a full update.

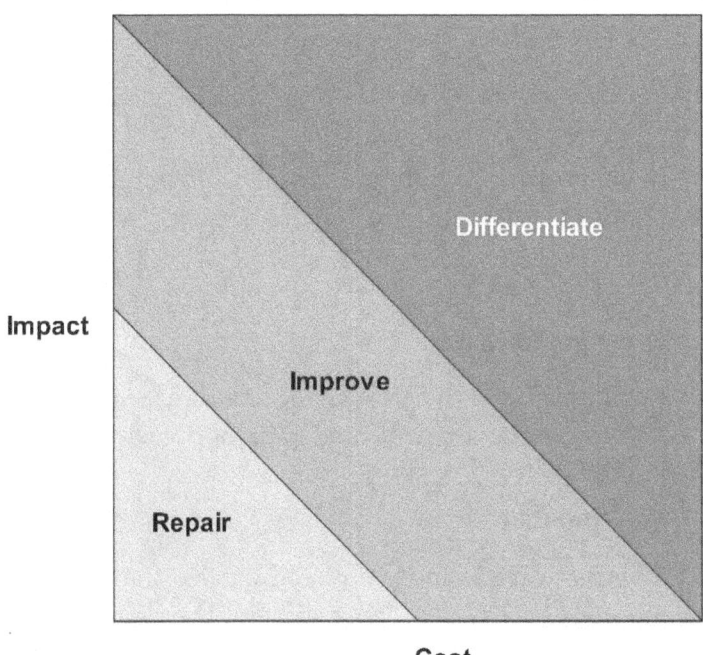

The cost and impact of repairing, improving and differentiating your product.

This diagram serves to remind us that the quickest and cheapest task is to fix existing problems in your product. Once that's done, you can add improvements. Finally, you should be seeking to differentiate your product from those of your competitors. Each step takes longer and is more expensive.

ACQUIRE A BUSINESS

If you have money in the bank and a line of credit, acquiring another business is a quick way to grow. Opportunistic acquisitions occur when a competitor is failing or has gone bust. Such businesses can often be bought cheaply.

This is often seen as a job for finance people, but what do they know about niches and market fit? Here are the main reasons why you'd want to buy a business.

1. Get more market share

Gobbling a competitor simply gives you a bigger share of the market. The more of them you buy, the more you dominate the market.

2. Expand geographically

You buy a company in a country or region where you'd like to operate. And you have a ready-made springboard.

3. Acquire Expertise

The tech companies routinely buy companies that have gee-whizz technology, because at least some of them will succeed. It shops the little company becoming a challenger in years to come, and it lets the giant understand the new technology.

4. Share cost

Some industries have heavy fixed costs, such as airlines. It makes sense to share landing spots, hangers, engineers and software.

5. Integrate vertically

You buy one of your suppliers or distributors. It gives you

better access to raw materials or customers.

6. Get into adjacent markets

If you sell fruit, you could buy a veg business. If you rent cars, you could buy a scooter rental company. The gap is small enough to reduce the risk, and it broadens your appeal.

7. It's a bargain

A distressed business is likely to go cheap. You may want to get it before your competitors do. That's the opportunistic purchase.

But acquisition isn't something to be undertaken lightly. Let's consider the benefits and risks.

Benefits

1. **Increased market share**: By acquiring a competitor, you can increase its market share, making the business more competitive. When Amazon acquired Whole Foods for $13.7 billion, it gave Amazon to Whole Foods' loyal customer base and brick-and-mortar stores, enabling Amazon to expand into the grocery industry and challenge the retail grocers.

2. **Access to new customers**: Acquiring a business can give you access to a new customer base, potentially increasing revenue and profit.

3. **Diversification**: If you acquire a company in a related industry, it lets you diversify your revenue streams and reduce reliance on a single product or service. In 2019, Disney acquired 21st Century Fox, which provided Disney with access to Fox's vast library of content, enabling it to diversify its offerings and compete with Netflix and other

streaming services.

4. **Cost savings**: You can reduce costs by combining operations and reducing duplication. You may need only one operating site, and you can remove a tier of management.

Disadvantages

1. **Integration problems**: Merging two companies can be challenging, particularly in terms of integrating different cultures and operations.

2. **Financial risks**: Acquiring a business can be expensive and may require taking on debt, which can be a financial risk. When Microsoft bought Nokia's mobile phone business for $7.2 billion, the acquisition was a financial failure, and the company was forced to write off $7.6 billion in losses.

3. **Regulatory hurdles**: Acquiring a business may require regulatory approval, which is time-consuming and uncertain. When WeWork attempted to buy its competitor, Regus, the deal fell apart due to regulatory concerns and the potential impact on competition in the co-working space.

4. **Damage to company reputation**: If you buy a business with a poor reputation or questionable business practices, you'll damage your own reputation. Uber acquired the ride-hailing startup, Otto, in an effort to enter the self-driving car market. But the acquisition was marred by legal disputes with Google's Waymo over alleged theft of intellectual property, which damaged Uber's reputation.

FIND YOUR BLUE OCEAN

I'm reluctant to include the Blue Ocean Strategy in a book on tactics, because it's a perfect example of a nebulous marketing strategy. It's the very thing I complained about at the start of this book.

It's a simple idea with a catchy title; but for most of us it's unlikely to produce practical results.

Blue Ocean Strategy is a book by Mauborgne and Chan Kim. I've summarized it briefly in the table below.

Red Ocean	Blue Ocean
Compete in existing markets	Create uncontested market space
Make a trade-off between cost and value	Break the cost – value trade-off
Beat the competition	Make the competition irrelevant

But maybe it could give you food for thought? Throw the rule book out of the window. Ignore the competition. Find an entirely new way of doing things. The trouble is, that's easier said than done. Here are two ways to find that blue ocean:

1. **It already exists out there**. Every new business idea already exists, somewhere. It will be badly executed, by an underfunded business, in a market that's not ready for it. All you have to do is find it, and then execute it properly.

2. **Look for markets that are ripe for disruption**. They have clunky systems, typically with gate-keeping intermediaries.

GRAB SOME MORE LAND

A land grab is all about scaling fast, with the aim of becoming the biggest player in the market. It's about grabbing market share before everyone else does.

Once you've achieved a pre-eminent position, you'll have acquired the majority of users, and thus lock out the competition – the so-called network effect. So, the aim of land grab is to pursue users, not profit.

Investors are constantly looking for the next big thing, and will invest huge sums of money in what they hope will be the market leader; and that in turn allows the business to staff up and continue advertising. This often lets the company acquire users at below cost, which can carry on for years.

Between 2011 and 2020, after 32 rounds of funding, Uber raised $25 billion, but lost money in each year except 2018 – when it managed to scrape in a tiny profit.

Few of us have the skills or network to harvest billions of dollars like Uber. And we may not be in the kind of niche that attracts flocks of investors. But we can still make a land grab if we are so minded.

Typically, a land grab is for a new market (for which, see Blue Ocean, above); and that often denotes a digital service taking over from manual.

But it can also be in markets dominated by lots of small, family-owned businesses. Examples of this include coffee shops, where Starbucks and its lookalikes sought to have a presence in every main street, leading to the closure of small independent coffee shops.

The main risks to a land grab

Churn: Your product has to meet a need and be superior to the competition. Otherwise, your customers will try your product for a while and leave. This leaves you constantly wooing new users.

Lack of profit. Land grab businesses have a cash runway. It's the length of time you have before your cash runs out. Investors will stay with you only for as long as they believe in you and your dream. Eventually, if you don't deliver, they will cash out.

How to execute a land grab

1. Identify a pioneer market. This requires foresight. You'll have to scan the horizon, and be aware of trends.

2. Set out to obtain category ownership. That is, be like eBay in online auctions or Walmart in retail (6,000 stores and a turnover of $250 billion). If you aren't number one or two, you'll fail.

3. Don't get distracted by other categories. Say focused.

4. Be prepared to invest in acquiring customers for years, without making profits. That will require investors, and so you need to be able to manage both your business and the ever-questioning financiers.

EXTEND INTO NEIGHBORING CATEGORIES

If you make soap bars, why not put the same branding on to shower gel? Or anti-antiperspirant? For not much effort, you get more facings on the supermarket or pharmacy shelves and knock back competitors.

Expanding your product into new categories or markets adds revenue and lets you find new customers. You leverage the brand recognition and customer loyalty that you've already built.

One of the main reasons why businesses opt for category extensions is to tap into new markets and customer segments. For example, if a business has a strong brand presence in the snacks market, it may decide to expand into the beverage market to reach a new set of customers.

This can help to increase sales and grow the business by offering new products to existing customers, as well as attracting new customers who may be interested in the brand.

Another benefit of a category extension is that it can help you diversify your product portfolio, reducing the risk associated with relying on a single product or market. By expanding into new categories, you can mitigate the impact of market changes and shifts in consumer preferences, which helps to ensure long-term sustainability. McDonald's moved into the café market with its McCafé brand. It plans 1,000 locations in China alone.

And a line extension can help you increase brand recognition and customer loyalty. By leveraging the reputation and trust that your brand has already built, you can create new products that are likely to be well-received by customers.

But it doesn't always succeed. After only three years of existence, Nike shut down its FuelBand fitness tracker. On paper, it made sense – with Nike well known for fitness and competitive sport. But the world is full of failed new product development, so there's no shame in new product failure.

And some are intended to be short-term wins, just to get media coverage. Oreo teamed up with Mondelez to create Oreo Ritz crackers. And then there was the Neapolitan, an ice cream Oreo with vanilla, strawberry, and chocolate colors. It pays to think outside the box.

A word of warning: ill-considered category extensions can dilute the brand identity and lose you customer loyalty.

Re-brand or re-package

Is your brand image or your packaging looking tired? A quick re-design can spruce it up. Here are three advantages:

- **Increased appeal**: Re-packaging can help you reach new target markets by adjusting the packaging to appeal to the specific preferences of these customers. Coca-Cola re-launched its diet soda in slimmer cans to appeal to health-conscious consumers.

- **Renewed interest in the brand**: Re-packaging can revive interest in an existing brand and make it seem fresh and new again. Tropicana re-branded its packaging to be more vibrant and modern to revive interest in the brand.

- **Cost savings**: Re-packaging can often be done at a lower cost than developing an entirely new brand, as the existing brand recognition and reputation can be leveraged.

This applies not just to the brand itself. Websites are surprisingly fashion-driven, and can quickly look dated. At one time, many websites had a scrolling carousel, which was hailed as the 'must-have' feature. Now they've all gone.

But there are risks in re-packaging a brand:

- **Loss of brand recognition**: If the re-packaging is too different from the original packaging, it can cause confusion among customers and lead to a loss of brand recognition. The relaunch of New Coke by Coca-Cola in 1985 was met with widespread criticism, and the original formula was quickly brought back.

- **Alienate existing customers**: Re-packaging can also alienate existing customers who are used to and fond of the original packaging.

How to implement a refresh

1. Carry out research to identify quantitatively whether a re-packaging is necessary.

2. Identify suitable designers and commission one.

3. Carry out research to evaluate consumer response to the new imagery.

4. Implement the new designs.

LICENSING

Rather than create your own product from scratch, it can be faster and simpler to license one from a business that already providing it.

This can give you access to a new niche and reduce your R&D costs. You leverage another company's technology or product to expand your own product range, without having to invest in the time and money it will require.

Japanese car maker Toyota licensed its hybrid technology to the Chinese car maker BYD. This allowed BYD to enter the Japanese market and produce hybrid cars under the Toyota brand, which had a strong reputation for quality and reliability.

Gilead Sciences licensed a pre-clinical oncology program from Scholar Rock, a biotechnology company. The licensing agreement meant Gilead could expand its potential cancer treatments without having to incur the costs and risks associated with developing a new drug.

And audio equipment company Sonos licensed technology from Google to enable voice control for its speakers. By partnering with Google, Sonos was able to enhance its brand as a high-quality, innovative product that integrates with popular smart home devices.

There are risks to both sides, however. If you license your product to another business, you give them access to your technology and could potentially lose your customers to them. And if you license another company's technology, you have to pay them royalties for as long as you sell that product, and you don't get to build your own expertise.

Simpler examples

If on the other hand, you're a toy maker, you can go to Walt Disney, Warner Bros, or Universal Pictures, and ask them to give you the rights to reproduce their latest blockbuster hero characters as dolls. In fact, licensed toy sales account for 30% of all toy sales. Such a partnership benefits both parties, because the film studios don't want to make toys and vice versa.

55 licensees produce Guinness-branded food and merchandise. The food includes boldly flavored brats (German sausages), meatballs, fish, chocolate and chips (crisps in UK English).

Songs are often licensed to TV shows and commercials. And luxury brands allow other businesses to use their logo. I have a pair of rugged boots with a Land Rover emblem on them. But here again, things can go wrong. Ralph Lauren's brand identity was cheapened by licensing cheap polo shorts.

PREDATORY THINKING

In his book Predatory Thinking, legendary ad man Dave Trott said he felt some of his clients weren't part of the serious business of marketing; of taking share from their competitors:

"They just want to make a nice commercial that everyone likes. Or do some nice online films that might go a little bit viral. Something that everyone quite likes. But nothing too controversial. Not messages that will upset the competition. Not anything that will make anyone uncomfortable.

"They don't really want to make waves. They don't want to cause a fuss. They don't really want to fight. Which suggests they're in the wrong job.

"Because marketing, like war, is a zero-sum game. If you want something, you have to take it from someone else.

"In order for someone to win, someone has to lose.... Everyone has to choose. Do they want to be the predator or the prey? Because, if they don't choose, the choice gets made for them."

Gosh, that's pretty uncompromising. Maybe it should come with a trigger warning?

Note that Dave treats only his competitors as prey, not his staff or his clients. Nor does he say you should break the law, be unethical, or run misleading ads. That's an important point. You just play to win.

As an ad man, Trott focuses on what will persuade consumers to buy his client's product.

And as a marketing person, you have a bigger canvas. You can use all the tools in this book to reach your customers, and those of your competitors, each and every day.

In his book, 'If you're in a dog fight, become a cat!' Leonard Sherman says: "Businesses often find themselves trapped in a competitive dogfight, scratching and clawing for market share with products consumers view as largely undifferentiated."

Rather than joining the dogfights within their industry, the solution, he says, is to be a cat, do things differently and be more innovative than the group of stupid dogs who spend time fighting each other rather than looking forward.

IT MAY BE OK TO BE A FOLLOWER

It's tiring being an innovator. You're having to constantly spend time dreaming up new ideas that mostly fail.

How much simpler it would be to see what works and adopt it. You don't even need your own manufacturing facilities or designers. There are plenty of businesses on Alibaba that will be delighted to create a look-alike product for you. There are food factories or toiletries businesses that churn out almost identical products, just with a different label.

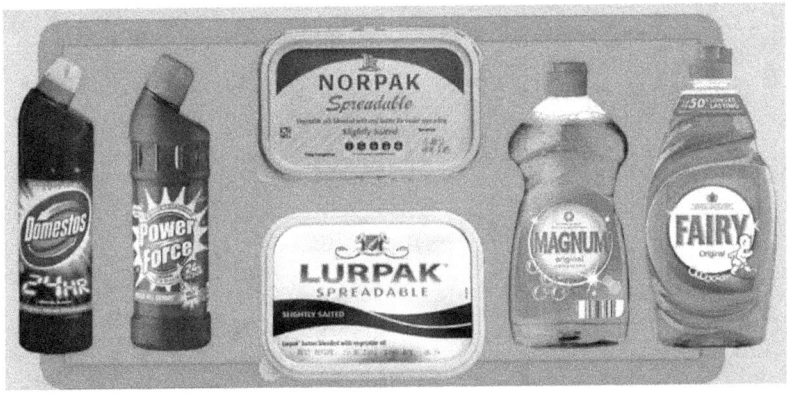

The Aldi supermarket chain has look-alike copies of branded products.

You can also benefit by offering complementary products or services to complement the offerings of market leaders. If the vacuum cleaner market leader sells expensive dust bags, you could offer your own, assuming you don't break the law.

Being a follower works if you have a range of products, and you add items to pad out your range. Maybe you sell cooking implements. Check what your competitors are selling, and add them to your range. They'll increase your revenue.

But being a follower carries its risks. You lack a unique selling proposition (USP). There's nothing unique about your product. Customers see you as a 'me-too'. You risk simply competing on price, and that way lies losses.

We're going to move on to examine planning in marketing. But first a request from the author:

Have you found this book useful so far?

If so, please give it a short review on Amazon. Just a few lines will do, and it should only take a couple of minutes.

Here's the link: https://mybook.to/tactical-marketing

Or point the camera on your phone at the QR code.

Your review matters more than you know, because it will help others find the book.

If you leave a review, be sure to let me know at KitSadgrove@gmail.com

> The reason everybody likes planning is that
> nobody has to do anything.
> - Jerry Brown

3. PLANNING TACTICS

ESCAPE YOUR INDUSTRY LIFE CYCLE

Most industries go through a life cycle, from birth, though growth, into maturity, and sometimes decay. Take the media:

- Around 60% of the US population went to the movies in the 1940s, declining to around 10% in recent years.

- Radio, by contrast, has held on to its audience, standing at around 80% of Americans aged over 12, through podcasting is a threat.

- UK newspapers have been in decline since as early as the mod 1950s, with the growth of alternative media.

So, what stage is your industry at? By reviewing the maturity of your products, you can better understand its current position and take advantage of opportunities or address the challenges.

Some threats are unexpected. Kodak was a name on every main street until digital photography arrived.

By contrast, IBM, originally known for its mainframe computers in the 1960s, skipped into personal computers as networking and cheap chips arrived. PC clones then started to reduce the profit on PCs, and IBM has since moved into cloud computing, AI and consulting. But in each decade its core markets started to fail, with its 1993 losses exceeding $8 billion.

How to avoid ending up in decline

1. Use scenario planning or horizon scanning to see what's coming.

2. Diversify your product portfolio to reduce dependence on mature products.

3. Innovate and improve existing products to maintain your competitiveness.

4. Enter new, growing markets.

5. Acquire or partner with companies in related or complementary industries.

ERECT BARRIERS TO ENTRY

If you have a dominant position in the market, you'll want to protect it against invaders, just as kings and barons did in the past. And just like in the past, one defensive method is to create barriers to entry. In the old days, you could dig a moat that made it hard for invaders to cross. These days, you have other options. Here are the main ones:

1. **Patents and Intellectual Property**: Patents and trademarks will prevent new entrants from producing similar products, and give you exclusive rights to sell the product. This might involve technology that makes you more productive or lets you provide a better service to customers.

2. **Build Networks**: If you have a large customer base and strong brand recognition, you can use that network to your advantage, making it difficult for new entrants to compete. This could include distributors, wholesalers or retailers, though you risk falling foul of competition laws.

3. **Regulation**: Government regulations and policies can create barriers to entry by making it difficult for new businesses to comply with regulations and enter the market. Savvy businesses sometimes encourage greater regulation. In the USA, interior designers have made it a requirement to pass interior design exams, something that discourages newcomers.

4. **Winner takes all**. In markets like online platforms, users congregate in the biggest provider. That's because it has the most comprehensive content, or has the greatest number of users they can interact with. You don't have to aspire to be Facebook: many smaller platforms grab a large chunk of their users, an example being McCormick's FlavorPrint, which assesses the user's tastes and palate, gives them a "flavor fingerprint," like a Myers-Briggs assessment, and then offers personalized recommendations for recipes.

5. **Distribution and Logistics**. Amazon has built a vast distribution network and logistics infrastructure, making it difficult for new entrants to compete in terms of delivery speed and reach.

6. **Economies of scale**: A business that is producing at a large scale can produce goods at a lower cost than a new entrant, making it difficult for them to compete on price. That said, low price is a difficult position to maintain, as someone will always try to undercut you.

HOW TO DEFINE YOUR COMPETITIVE ADVANTAGE

Every business has its competitors. So, why do people buy from you rather than from other businesses? The answer lies in your competitive advantage. It's the thing that makes you stand out, whether that's low price, exclusivity, wide range, proximity, or friendly service.

And yet, many businesses open shop every day without asking themselves that more basic of questions: why come to us?

If you don't understand your competitive advantage, you risk losing it through neglect. Whereas, if you *are* familiar with it, you can protect it, magnify it, enhance it, and promote it to prospects.

Here are some common competitive advantages:

- **Cost**: Can you reduce the cost of production or by finding ways to produce the same quality goods or services at a lower cost? Walmart has created a cost advantage by using its massive buying power to negotiate lower prices from suppliers, and by streamlining its supply chain operations. But emphasizing low prices can risk a downward race into making a loss.

- **Design**: Good design means different things in different markets. In one niche, it might be ease of use. In another, it could be the product's appearance. Apple has differentiated itself from other tech companies by offering a premium user experience and a sleek, stylish design.

- **Process**: You may use proprietary technologies that others don't have access to.

- **Focus**: A local chain of glass merchants cuts and supplies all kinds of glass for all kinds of purposes. If I need glass, I know who to go to.

- **Innovate**: You can introduce new products, services or processes that are significantly better than what is currently available in the market.

- **Customer Service**: Providing excellent customer service can be a significant source of competitive advantage.

- **Reputation**: Building a strong brand reputation can help you attract customers who are looking for a particular level of quality and trustworthiness.

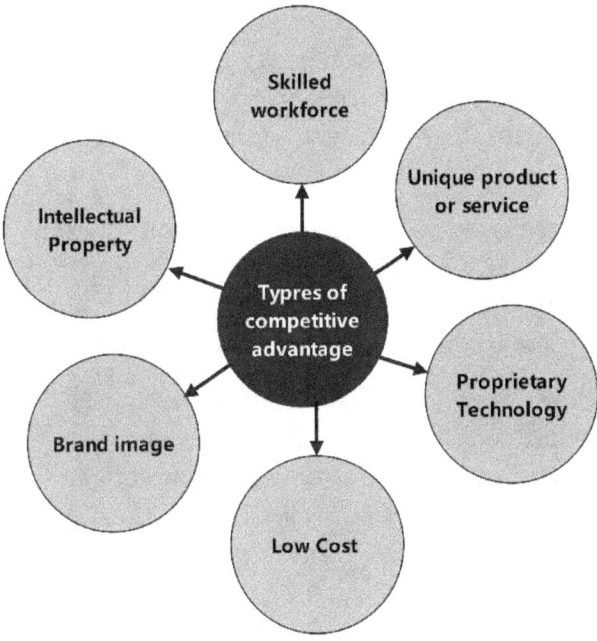

Six types of competitive advantage

How to define your competitive advantage

1. **Identify** what brings customers to you, rather than to your competitors.

2. **Enhance and nurture** that advantage.

3. **Communicate** your advantage to customers and prospects.

4. **Maintain** the advantage by innovating and adapting to changes in the market.

WHERE IS YOUR GAP?

You can use Gap Analysis to identify the differences between your current state and where to want to be, with the aim of closing the gap.

In terms of sales and customer engagement, gap analysis can help you identify areas for improvement, prioritize initiatives, and ultimately increase your sales and customer engagement.

You might use gap analysis to compare your current customer satisfaction levels with the levels you would prefer. You can then identify the factors contributing to the gap, such as a lack of personalization in the customer experience or poor product quality.

Gap Analysis could help you review your current sales process with what it could be. This could include longer sales cycles, lack of qualified leads, or low close rates. By addressing these areas, you can improve its sales process and ultimately increase its sales.

Some Metrics to consider

- Website traffic
- Bounce rates
- Number of subscribers
- Advertising click-through rates
- Cost per acquisition

- Customer churn

- Revenue growth

- Revenue per sales person

How to close the gaps

1. Identify the current state of your sales or marketing, particularly in terms of metrics.

2. Compare your metrics with industry averages, if available.

3. Decide what you want it to be.

4. Identify the gaps this reveals.

5. Devise improvements to close the gaps.

6. Set up a system to record progress.

7. Allocate resources to implement the plan.

THE FLYWHEEL AND THE DOOM LOOP

The flywheel is a metaphor about constantly making small improvements, rather than pursuing the next shiny object. In his book Good to Great, Jim Collins says:

> No matter how dramatic the end result, good-to-great transformations never happen in one fell swoop. In building a great company or social sector enterprise, there is no single defining action, no grand program, no one killer innovation, no solitary lucky break, no miracle moment. Rather, the process resembles relentlessly pushing a giant,

heavy flywheel, turn upon turn, building momentum until a point of breakthrough, and beyond.

This may not be entirely true. Microsoft got a lucky break when IBM asked them to create the operating system for its PCs - and gave them the rights to put it on other machines. That was the one breakthrough upon which the company is based. But it is true that any established business only stays in the race if it continuously improves. It's similar to Kaizen: you achieve continuous improvement by making small positive changes.

Anyway, back to the flywheel. It's a device that stores rotational energy. It takes a lot of energy to get a flywheel started, but as it picks up speed it begins to spin by itself. You can feel that in a car. Going from zero to 15mph takes effort, but once on the highway it bowls along. Inertia keeps it going.

The flywheel is different from the *marketing funnel*. The flywheel assumes you have to keep moving and improving, or you slow to a halt. It also assumes a loop, either positive or negative, which either builds momentum or acts as a drag.

By contrast, the tunnel implies you simply drop prospects in at the top and some will convert. It's linear, whereas the flywheel is circular.

The more friction on the flywheel, the less likely it will spin freely. So, your task is to remove the difficulties that prospects encounter, for instance by providing warranties.

Collins calls for businesses to focus on their customers, understand their needs, and concentrate on delivering a great product and service.

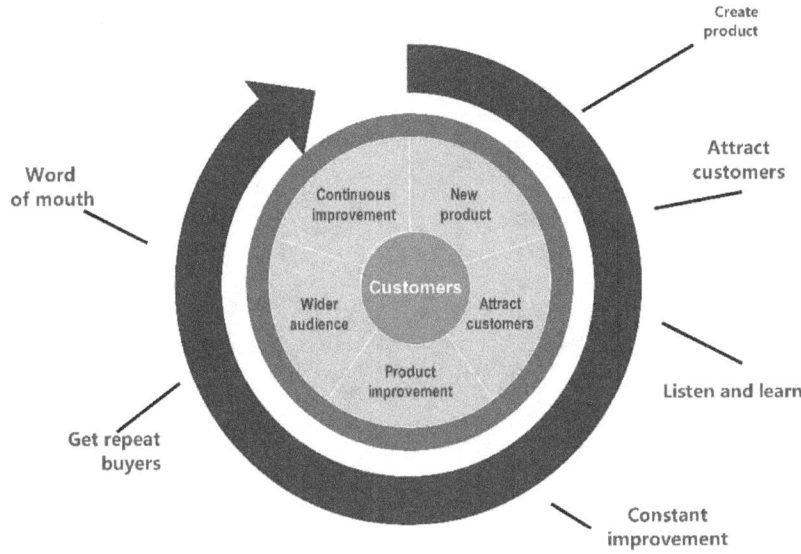

The Flywheel

The flywheel works for tactical marketing

The flywheel concept aligns with this book. Taking regular steps to communicate with your customers, get feedback, improve your product, and do promotion to attract more people - that sounds pretty tactical and effective.

Most marketing isn't about re-inventing the wheel. It's about showing up every day and improving incrementally.

Collins suggests that many businesses react badly to changing circumstances. They fail to understand what's going on, and respond by running promotions or cutting prices, and end up in a declining path, what Collins called the Doom Loop.

Disappointing results

Management fails to understand

No momentum

Management introduces new direction, new CEO, acquisition, marketing...

The Doom Loop

CONCENTRATE?

There are advantages in concentrating on a particular market or industry segment.

By specializing in a specific area, you position your business as an expert in its field and thereby gain a competitive advantage.

A concentration strategy allows you to create economies of scale, leading to lower production costs, increased efficiency and higher profit margins. And it means management doesn't get distracted.

The athletic clothing brand Lululemon sells only high-quality yoga wear, mostly for women. This has helped the company differentiate itself from its competitors, and create a loyal customer base that's willing to pay a premium for its products.

Starbucks focuses on providing premium coffee and espresso-based drinks to its customers. By specializing in this area, Starbucks has been able to create a unique brand identity and develop a strong customer following. It has also allowed the company to expand its product offerings and create new revenue streams, such as its food and merchandise lines.

But there are risks. It can attract lookalikes which produce a similar product at a lower price. Your niche can become unfashionable or crowded.

And if you become a monopoly, the government might step in. The US Department of Justice has long alleged that Google has "engaged in a course of anti-competitive and exclusionary conduct that consisted of neutralizing or eliminating ad tech competitors through acquisitions; wielding its dominance across digital advertising markets to force more publishers and advertisers to use its products; and thwarting the ability to use competing products."

So, concentration can be great when you're growing. But at some point, you might want to diversify, which is what we look at next.

See also: "Adopt the 80/20 Rule".

OR DIVERSIFY?

If you're worried about your market declining or becoming unduly competitive, you might be considering diversification.

That would let you expand into new products or markets or products. In doing so, you would reduce the risk associated with dependence on a single product or market, and create new revenue streams.

That decision to diversify can be driven by various factors, such as changes in the market, technological advances, competition, or customer preferences.

You might diversify when your current products or market

are reaching saturation or decline, and there is limited growth potential. Additionally, diversification can help you leverage your existing capabilities and resources to enter new markets or create new products.

Amazon started as an online bookseller but later expanded into other product categories, such as electronics, clothing and, later, groceries. It even created new revenue streams through services like Amazon Web Services and Prime Video.

And Alphabet, the parent company of Google, started as a search engine but went into other businesses such as cloud computing. This helped Alphabet reduce its dependence on search advertising.

But you need to ensure you have the necessary skills and resources to support a new venture. And there is always the risk of failing to focus on what you do best.

Automate your marketing

How much of your marketing is manual? While people are essential for creating new activity (as you're doing in having bought this book), and interacting with customers, automation has a big role to play.

Chat: Even the simplest of chat systems gives you one more way for customers to read you. And when you don't have staff to respond to a chat request, it can save a customer's message.

Chatbots: AI-powered chatbots can provide 24/7 customer support, answer frequently asked questions, and assist customers with their purchases.

Autoresponders allow you to maintain a relationship with prospects and customers by sending personalized newsletters and emails at regular intervals. It can also respond to predetermined triggers, for example by sending a welcome email to new subscribers or a follow-up email after a purchase.

If a prospect hasn't opened an email after a certain number of days, the system can send a follow-up email or a special offer to re-engage the prospect, as the Boden example below shows. As such, they carry out work that a human would not have the time to do.

This behavior-based approach helps to personalize the customer experience and can lead to higher conversion rates. If you're a Pizza Hut customer, you may get a free offer on your birthday.

CRM (customer relationship management) software will track the company's dialogue with customers, their changing personnel, and their developing needs.

Shopping basket abandonment is another area where marketing automation can help businesses. The machine can determine when a customer has added items to their cart but has not completed the purchase. It can then trigger a series of reminder emails to entice the customer into completing their purchase.

Boden follow-up popup

How to automate your marketing

1. Identify what tasks are being done manually. Look out for people using ring binders, legal pads, and paper-based to-do lists.

2. Note where friction takes place in your sales and marketing process. What errors, complaints, and returns are occurring? Where do customers seem to have questions or problems?

3. See whether automated systems could obviate these problems.

4. Commission an individual or project team to implement and launch your tools.

ADAPT YOUR MARKETING TO LOCAL CIRCUMSTANCES

We're supposed to be living in a globalized world. But the more homogenized we get, the more that people want to cling to their local traditions. That's not surprising. Many feel unnerved about the pace of change and the loss of their culture.

So, adapting marketing strategies to suit local conditions can help you increase your sales.

This means adjusting the marketing mix (product, price, place and promotion) to cater to the cultural, economic, and demographic differences of each market. And you should also consider the local language, regulations and communication channels.

In Asia, Coca-Cola introduced green tea-flavored drinks to suit local tastes. In India, it launched smaller packs at lower prices to suit the country's price-sensitive market. McDonald's has offered a vegetarian McAloo Tikki burger in India.

For digital products, it may be as simple as making them

available in different languages.

However, there can be problems. Localization may increase costs. And it can cause problems if local management starts to stray too far from the international product. But this can be resolved by having a design or communication manual and enforcing it. Major businesses sometimes appoint a global ad agency, knowing that the agency's head office will keep its regional branches in order.

How to adapt to local conditions

1. Identify though research or field visits whether the preferences of local markets vary from what you offer.

2. Evaluate the costs and risks of creating local versions of your product.

3. Where suitable, create localized solutions.

CHANGE YOUR POSITIONING

Positioning is the process of creating a unique image and identity in the customer's mind for a business or its products, with the goal of making them stand out from competitors and appealing to target customers.

Here are some of the main ways you can position itself to boost sales and increase customer loyalty:

- **Market Segmentation**: By identifying and focusing on specific groups of customers, you can tailor your products, marketing and customer service to meet the specific needs and preferences of each segment. Nike targets athletes and fitness enthusiasts, while Apple targets tech-savvy consumers.

- **Unique Selling Proposition (USP)**: A USP is a unique

benefit or feature that sets a business or its products apart from the competition. Coca-Cola positions itself as the drink that brings people together, while Dyson positions itself as a technology company that solves problems with innovation.

- **Brand Image and Identity**: Building a strong brand image and identity can help create an emotional connection with customers and establish trust and loyalty. Porsche is known for its high-performance sports cars, and Rolex is known for its luxury watches.

- **Price Positioning**: By positioning its products at a certain price point, you can appeal to different target customer segments based on your budget and expectations. For example, Walmart appeals to budget-conscious customers, while Tiffany & Co. appeals to customers who are willing to pay a premium price for luxury products.

- **Customer Experience**: Providing a positive customer experience, including quality products and customer service, can increase customer loyalty and help position a business as a customer-focused company. For example, Zappos is known for its exceptional customer service and easy returns.

In conclusion, positioning is a key aspect of marketing that can help you differentiate your business from the competition and appeal to target customers. By using a combination of these strategies, you can boost sales and increase customer loyalty.

How to re-position the business

1. Identify through research:

   - The benefits sought after by customers.

- Your brand positioning versus your competitors.

2. Commission an agency to translate your findings into a creative execution, or set up a competition for a new strapline or catch-phrase.

3. Implement the phrase and look across your marketing materials

FIND OUT WHERE YOU ADD VALUE

The net profit margin for food processors is 5%. But for drinks producers, both alcoholic and non-alcoholic, such as Scotch whisky and Coca-Cola, it's 15%.

This suggests you'll make very little money from producing raw materials, whereas selling branded, value-added goods is highly profitable.

To an extent, this looks like an argument for moving up the supply chain. Don't grow coffee beans: buy the beans and turn them into coffee pods.

But that's not the real story. The task is to add value.

If you're selling basic products that are undifferentiated from those of other businesses, you're vulnerable. Customers who can buy the same product or service from many suppliers will do so at the lowest possible price.

There are some quirks in the data. Grocery stores operate on wafer-thin margins of 2%, but they can live with that as long as they maintain their huge volumes. Businesses in declining markets such as newspapers may have differentiated products (compare the Wall Street Journal with the New York Post) but their margins will be slim.

So it's about making your product more worthwhile to your customers. It may mean abandoning some low-value sector that you currently serve, and moving into higher value areas.

You can conduct a Value Chain Analysis (VCA) by identifying each step of your business activities, and assessing which of them create value for your customers.

Design is a big part of the solution, whether that's in the product or the service; and we're talking about meaningful, functional design, not just imagery.

How to add value

1. Assess the elements that your customers value most. Do they want fast delivery, an ethical profile, confidentiality, or some other requirement?

2. Identify each step in your process, and determine how much value they provide to the customer, or provide some benefit to the business (such as a unique technology or method).

3. Understand the common points you share with your competitors. On which aspects are you all alike?

4. Now assess how you can add value and distinguish your business from all the rest.

HIT AND RUN

The essence of "Hit and Run" is short-term activity. You launch and advertise a product to take advantage of a seasonal trend, and then withdraw it. This might be a summer- or Christmas-based product where you expect revenue will be high, but for only a limited period.

And if you're in a fashion-led market, you would launch this season's fad, and get ready to stop it when consumers move on to the next big thing. Onesies, crop tops, UGG boots, tiny sunglasses - the fashions keep arriving and departing.

Or you want to increase visibility in a crowded market, so you set up a popup store.

Hit and Run works well in markets where the barriers to entry are low. You can create a new product, see if it works, and pull it if sales don't materialize. The advantage is that you get to try plenty of opportunities at relatively low cost.

Hit and Run is also practical in markets where your competitors are asleep at the wheel, and are unlikely to retaliate. As with other tactics in this book, the aim is to try new things and stay one step ahead.

So, you don't have to be Al Capone to use hit and run tactics. It's perfectly acceptable to try new things and be ready to pull them quickly if they don't succeed. Maybe we need a less aggressive phrase for this tactic?

Next, we'll be looking at competitor tactics

Competitors are the one thing that stands between you and your customer. So if you can dislodge them, re-position them, or simply be better than them, the way is clear to making more revenue. Let's look at how to do that.

Business is war. I go out there, I want to kill the competitors. I want to make their lives miserable. I want to steal their market share. I want them to fear me and I want everyone on my team thinking we're going to win.

- Kevin O'Leary

4. COMPETITOR TACTICS

BENCHMARK YOUR COMPETITORS

Most of us have a view on how we compare against our competitors. Maybe we know competitor A's product has a bigger market share, better features or a lower price. But do we do anything about that? All too often, we accept the status quo.

Competitive benchmarking forces us to review the strengths and weaknesses of our competitors, and improve what we do as a result. It aims to identify what others are doing better, and adopt those practices.

It's an aid to decision-making, because it gives us focused answers that help in product development, pricing and marketing. And it provides an insight into what makes other businesses successful, and thus helps us stay competitive.

A case in point is United Airlines which wanted to improve its website, to make it easier for customers to book flights online. So it compared its site against several of its competitors. This involved fifty-two testing sessions in two phases. As a result of the findings and the changes it made, United was able to increase the site's effectiveness and customer satisfaction.

But there are pitfalls:

1. **It can be time-consuming and expensive**: benchmarking requires research and analysis, which can be time-consuming and costly.

2. **It's tempting to rank your business higher** than others. Independent evaluation is needed.

3. **It can lead to a 'copycat' mentality**: you may be tempted to adopt strategies or practices without considering their unique circumstances. This results in imitation rather than innovation. It's good practice to examine businesses in other industries. For example, a theme park could look at airports to assess queuing and customer flow.

4. **Benchmarking may not always be applicable to your specific situation**, leading to inaccurate comparisons and flawed decision-making. Maybe your main competitor has more resources or is longer established?

5. **The benchmarking process can become unwieldy**, lead simply to 'facts', and not result in improvements. An iterative and modular approach may produce better results.

Many organizations use a spreadsheet, like the one below. While this can provide a top-line numerical result, there's a risk that it won't provide insights. For that reason, qualitative research, using in-depth interviews or focus groups, may be more useful.

	Us	Competitor A	Competitor B	Competitor C
Speed of delivery	4	4	5	3
Function-ality	4	3	5	3
Product quality	4	3	4	2
Support	4	4	5	3
No. of outlets	3	5	4	2

Benchmarking matrix

How to benchmark

1. Identify your competitors and comparators.

2. Define the criteria to be evaluated. This should be based on factors known to influence consumer satisfaction (or whatever specific outcome you are seeking).

3. Carry out the research.

4. Review the findings.

5. Implement the improvements.

FLANK OR FRONTAL ATTACK?

If you want to attack a market sector, do you go for a full-on frontal attack, aiming to knock down an established, well-loved brand? You'd need deep pockets for that. And there's a high risk of failure. So it might be less costly, and allow a higher chance of success, if you went for a less obvious corner of the market. That's called a flank attack.

In a flank attack, you target a competitor's weak points to gain market share. The aim is to capture the market segments that are not well served by established companies.

A technology company might launch a flank attack on its competitor by offering a more user-friendly and affordable product. This can attract customers who are not satisfied with the complicated and expensive offerings of established companies. Canva makes inroads into Adobe design software products by lowering the skills needed.

For example, if you wanted to enter the food business, you might find that a particular regional or national cuisine has been overlooked by the existing competitors. So you could build a niche brand around Philippine flavors, Middle Eastern barbecue, or climate-conscious foods. This allows you to differentiate yourself and appeal to a new market segment.

You'll need to analyze the market and your competitors before executing a flank attack. This will help you identify the weak points and determine the best approach.

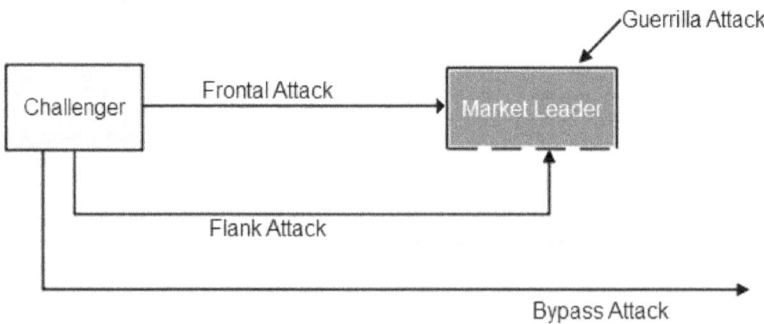

Frontal, Flank, Bypass and Guerrilla tactics

Options to avoid a front attack include a flank attack, guerrilla attack, or simply bypass the competition, using a Blue Ocean format.

HOW TO DEFEND YOUR POSITION

You're a market leader. The competitors are circling. They sense weakness, and they're aggressive. How do you defend your position? Here are four tactics.

- **Set up a barrier to entry**: This involves creating substantial costs or other obstacles that would discourage new entrants from entering the market. For example, Coca-Cola has established a strong distribution network that is difficult for new entrants to replicate.

- **Set up exclusive distribution contracts**: You might establish contracts with suppliers or distributors that prevent competitors from accessing the same distribution channels. Nike has exclusive partnerships with retailers like Foot Locker and Finish Line, making it difficult for competitors to reach the same level of distribution.

- **Create intellectual property rights**: This involves developing a particular technology, product, design or process, and then gaining exclusive rights to it, thereby preventing competitors from using the same ideas. This might be a patent, trade mark, copyright, recipe or trade secret. Louboutin has red soled shoes, while Google has an eye-watering 80,000 patents covering web search, cloud computing and display advertising.

- **Establish a brand image**: This involves creating a strong and recognizable brand that is associated with quality, reliability, and trust. For example, Procter & Gamble has built a strong brand image for its products, such as Tide laundry detergent and Crest toothpaste, which have become synonymous with quality in their respective categories.

Louboutin successfully defends its trademark red shoes, though these knock-offs cost only $3.53 (£2.99) on a well-known Chinese import website.

STRENGTHEN YOUR LINKS WITH INTERMEDIARIES

Unless you only sell direct, intermediaries will play an important role in distributing your products and services to your end customers.

This includes wholesalers, retailers, agents and distributors who help you reach your target market. Fostering and supporting your intermediaries can benefit you in several ways.

They will help to expand your reach, especially in new markets. By leveraging your existing relationships and networks, intermediaries can help you reach customers that would otherwise be difficult to access.

They also bring valuable knowledge and expertise to the table. Intermediaries will have insights into market trends and consumer behavior, helping you to refine your marketing and sales strategies.

Third, intermediaries can help to improve your overall customer experience. They're often the first point of contact for customers and can provide pre-sales support, answer customer questions, and resolve issues.

Finally, building a strong relationship will build loyalty. This would make your intermediaries less likely to de-list you or take on new competitors. It will also ensure that both parties understand the other's needs.

How to improve your relationship with intermediaries

1. Identify your biggest intermediaries, without overlooking smaller but nevertheless important ones.

2. Consider offering incentives such as commission-based compensation

3. Provide sales and product training

4. Ensure there is adequate marketing support.

5. Ensure regular communication takes place.

6. Set up collaborations, such as joint promotions.

7. Consider having hospitality events that mix business and pleasure. Being relaxed, such events can build relationships outside the office environment.

SIMPLY COPY WHAT OTHERS DO

Why spend time and money when you could adapt what existing brands do? It's a "me too" approach. You learn from what your competitor has taken years to develop, and copy it overnight. An internet entrepreneur once said, "Whatever someone launches online, I could copy in six weeks".

This strategy is often adopted by businesses looking to enter a market quickly, without having to invest significant resources in research and development or new product development.

In the smartphone market, many companies have adopted an imitative marketing strategy by copying the design and features of successful brands such as Samsung's Galaxy. This has allowed these companies to establish themselves and compete with established brands.

In the fast-food industry, many chains have copied the menu items, pricing, and marketing strategies of successful competitors such as McDonald's. This has allowed them to quickly gain a share of the market.

But while a copycat strategy can give you quick entry into a market, it may not always result in long-term success. And there's the risk of lawsuits and negative public perception. You may also struggle to gain consumer acceptance.

The main disadvantage is that you lack distinctiveness. So you'll need a USP to peel customers away from their current supplier. Occasionally, brute force works. For example, you might have a sales force that can muscle its way in; or you can outspend the reigning champ who doesn't think it's necessary to advertise.

How to copy what others are doing

1. Identify a market or niche you'd like to enter.

2. Research the needs of that market, such as functionality, pricing, margins, customer dissatisfactions, and levels of loyalty to existing products and companies.

3. Create your own product that matches or surpasses the necessary functions of existing products, and launch it.

AMBUSH YOUR COMPETITORS

This can be an aggressive tactic, but it's often done in a tongue-in-cheek way.

You can use ambush marketing to associate your brand with a major event, such as a sports event or a music festival - but without actually paying for official sponsorship. You'd hope to benefit from the increased exposure and positive association with the event, while avoiding the sponsorship costs.

For example, you might launch a marketing campaign that's similar in style and messaging to the official sponsor of an event. People would then associate you with the event.

Or you could have a marketing activity that takes place near the event, such as setting up a promotional booth near the venue or distributing flyers in the surrounding area. Here are three examples:

- Adidas was one of the official sponsors of the 2012 London Olympics. But in the period leading up to the games, Nike ran ads featuring Olympic athletes such as Mo Farah and Usain Bolt. The ads were timed to air just before the start of the Olympics, which gave Nike a major boost.

- At the 2016 Olympics, a Japanese restaurant set up a stall near the Olympic Village, offering free meals to athletes. The restaurant quickly became popular with athletes, many of whom posted about it on social media. As a result, the company got a lot of free publicity without having to pay for official sponsorships.

- In Santa Monica, California, Audi created a billboard with a picture of their new Audi A4 on it. The caption read, "Your move, BMW." The BMW dealership in the same area took out another billboard with a picture of their new BMW M3 Coupe. The caption on the BMW board read "Checkmate."

BMW ambush marketing

Ambush marketing can be effective for companies looking to increase awareness and sales, as it allows them to associate your brand with a major event and benefit from the increased exposure.

But note that ambush marketing is not always legal and can lead to negative consequences, such as damage to your brand reputation and legal action from event organizers or official sponsors.

How to ambush your competitors' activity.

1. Identify any major forthcoming events.

2. Decide how you could set up an ambush.

3. Weigh up the pros and cons of such activity.

4. If you decide to go ahead, create plans to implement the ambush.

GUERRILLA MARKETING

Guerrilla marketing is a creative and unconventional approach to promoting a product or service. Unlike traditional marketing methods, which rely heavily on advertising through mass media, guerrilla marketing uses surprise and unconventional tactics to reach a target audience. The goal is to create a buzz and generate word-of-mouth promotion.

Guerrilla marketing can take many forms, from street art to flash mobs to viral videos. One popular tactic is to create an event or spectacle in a public place that captures people's attention and gets them talking.

You might set up a pop-up shop in an unexpected location, like a subway station or a busy street corner. This creates a sense of surprise and intrigue; and people are more likely to remember the brand and tell their friends about it.

Or you might create an interactive experience that allows customers to engage with a brand in a new and exciting way. You could create a virtual reality experience that allows customers to explore a product or service in a new and exciting way. This creates an immersive experience and increased engagement that is likely to lead to word-of-mouth promotion.

Guerrilla marketing can be an effective way to reach a target audience, especially in today's digital age. With social media and the internet, word-of-mouth promotion can spread quickly and reach a large audience. But guerrilla marketing can be risky, as it relies heavily on surprise and unconventional tactics. If a campaign fails to capture people's attention or generate buzz, it can backfire and harm a brand's reputation. Here are some examples:

- Coca-Cola's "Share a Coke" campaign, where the company put popular names on its cans and bottles, encouraging customers to buy the drink for their friends with the same name.

- Nike's "Just Do It" slogan and logo plastered on city walls and sidewalks (pavements), creating an urban and edgy feel for the brand.

- IKEA's annual "Sleepover" event where customers were invited to spend the night in the store, creating a memorable and unique brand experience.

Nike encourages travelers to take the stairs!

Next we look at product tactics.

This ranges from identifying and communicating your USP (in case you haven't done that), to turning services into products.

We also look at fighting brands and limited-edition products.

Great companies are built on great products.
- Elon Musk

5. PRODUCT TACTICS

In this section, we look at how to maximize the value of your products.

It's all too easy to assume that your product is unchanging. But we know that people's needs change, competitors act, and the economy varies. We can also see how the top brands update their products over time. So let's examine how you can add value or improve the quality of what you offer.

What's your USP?

In Innovation Tactics, we discussed the 'competitive advantage'. One possible offshoot of that thought process is to codify it in a Unique Selling Proposition (USP), to which it's closely related.

A USP is a clear statement that distinguishes your product or service from that of your competitors. It highlights the special benefit it provides to your customers.

Creating a USP is a crucial step in establishing a unique and memorable brand identity.

It should be simple, memorable, and accurately reflect the

value that your company provides to its customers. A well-crafted USP can increase brand awareness, customer loyalty, and sales.

Death Wish Coffee tells us it's 'The World's Strongest Coffee'. It's an exclusive claim, which separates it from other coffees that major on flavor.

Meanwhile, the Asket fashion brand single-mindedly pursues its environmental credentials with 'The Pursuit of Less'.

The Asket website

How to create a USP

1. **Know your target market**: Understanding the needs, wants, and preferences of your target market is essential in developing a USP that appeals to them.

2. **Identify your company's strengths**: Evaluate your company's products or services, resources, and capabilities to

determine what sets you apart from your competitors.

3. **Conduct market research**: Analyze the market, competition, and customer feedback to identify the unmet needs in your industry.

4. **Formulate some USP statements**: Combine the insights from steps 1 to 3 to create a set of concise, compelling statements that convey the unique benefit your company provides.

5. **Test and implement**: Test your USPs in research, and choose the best.

CLARITY OF OFFER

Mercedes is well known for its upscale executive cars. But it also applies the brand name to its ordinary blue-collar vans. That's not so clever. When you see the Merc triangle on a van, you might think, "That doesn't look like a prestige vehicle. So, maybe Mercedes isn't so posh after all?"

Maintaining a "clarity of offer" is about keeping your product line simple and consistent with its brand identity. That's important because it helps establish and reinforce your brand image, making it easier for consumers to understand what you stand for and what products they can expect from them.

If you're known for producing high-quality sports equipment, you should avoid adding kitchen appliances. This would dilute your brand image and confuse customers. Similarly, you shouldn't sell cheap sports equipment for the same reason (though see Line or Category Extension).

The same applies to clarity of communication. Many businesses have a corporate communication and design manual to ensure that messaging is consistent.

By avoiding unsuitable line extensions and offloading products that do not align with your brand image, you can build a stronger and more recognizable brand. This, in turn, can increase consumer loyalty and help the business differentiate itself from its competitors.

THE GOLDEN GOOSE

The Golden Goose refers to the most important product or service in your business. It's the one that generates the most revenue or profit. It's the lifeblood of the business, and often the product for which you're best known. Other products (or 'shoulder brands') may develop from it.

The golden goose can take many forms. It can be a popular product that is in high demand, a service that is unique and sought after, or an idea that sets the company apart from its competitors.

The key to finding a golden goose is to identify what sets your business apart from your competitors and capitalize on that. If you're able to identify and nurture your golden goose, you can reap rewards in terms of revenue and profit.

Once identified, you must maintain its relevance and keep it up to date. A golden goose can lose its shine over time if you don't invest in research and development, and you fail to identify new trends and market needs. All too often we take it for granted because it's been around a long time.

Apple's iPhone is often referred to as the company's golden goose. The iPhone generates a significant portion of Apple's revenue and profit and is considered the company's most valuable product. Apple invests in research and development to ensure that the iPhone remains relevant.

Sprite, Lilt and Dr Pepper are all fine brands, but they don't compare with Coca-Cola, the company's original product, and the company's golden goose. A product like Coca-Cola allows the business the income to develop new products.

How to define and manage your Golden Goose.

1. Identify whether you have a 'Golden Goose'. It's your best-selling product, the one that generates the most income.

2. Commit to supporting and investing in your Golden Goose.

3. Ensure that all staff know they should put the majority of their effort into supporting the Golden Goose, not less important products (while not ignoring new contenders).

MAKE YOUR INTANGIBLES TANGIBLE

If you need freight forwarding, a repair service or a hairdresser, you can't test them in advance. You can read reviews or talk to users, but other people's experience may not reflect your specific needs.

You can test drive a car, but is it exactly the same model as you want? Will it be reliable? Will your friends and neighbors be impressed? You can inspect and test a drilling machine in the supplier's factory, but will they install it properly?

And this isn't limited to purely service businesses. Most products have some level of intangibility. If you put a completely unfamiliar wrapper on a Mars bar, few people would buy it.

As a result, we have to turn to proxies - things that suggest the product will be good. They include the following:

- Face-to-Face impressions. The first meeting, the handshake, the cup of coffee, how interest the vendor shows in the prospect.

- Brand history

- Reviews

- Communication and marketing. Some businesses use imagery and metaphors - images of happy families or a car snaking serenely through empty mountain roads.

- Samples and tests

- Product packaging - including for b2b products.

- Case studies

- Delivery. This can involve not just the process of delivering a package from one place to another, but also how long will it take you to build my new factory?

- Systemization of services. This can be routing of phone calls, training staff to perform routine activities, or providing efficient online access for customers.

- Support quality, which includes not just speed of response but also friendliness, follow up, monitoring of service levels, and even the look of the support materials such as chatbots or layout of emails.

- Stated values that indicate trustworthiness, such as a values statement.

- Community or charity engagement.

- Refunds and guarantees

- And when the sale is done, after sales is often important, because it affects word of mouth and repeat business.

These intangibles can add significant value to its offerings, and help set your company apart from your competitors.

For example, by highlighting its buyer experience, a company can show customers that it values their time and is committed to making their shopping experience as seamless and enjoyable as possible. This could include features such as free returns, 24/7 customer support, and a user-friendly website.

How to implement this tactic

1. Understand the customer's real wants and fears. What are they buying? Reliability? Sex appeal? Productivity?

2. What will put them off? New business sales people need to have emotional intelligence. Bankers need to exude reassurance - but not be condescending.

3. Build a set of indicators, as suggested in the list above.

LIMITED EDITIONS

Creating a limited edition of your product creates excitement and a sense of scarcity, which drives demand and increases sales.

Also known as a 'product drop' in some industries, it involves making a new product available for only a limited time or in limited quantities, creating a sense of exclusivity and urgency among consumers.

Consumers may feel that they need to act quickly to get their hands on the product or service, leading to increased purchases and revenue for the business.

This strategy can lead to increased word of mouth and chat on social media, which raises consumer awareness.

And a limited supply of anything often allows you to charge a premium price.

- Skater fashion brand Supreme Clothing has a limited number of retail stores in major cities. It releases mini-collections of stock, and allows it to completely sell out. They then close the shop doors until the next product drop. Supreme also has a similar tactic online. Every Thursday at 11am, a new mini-collection appears on its website, often selling out in a few hours.

- The Lay's snack company blends differ-ent flavors to create new limited-time products, such as Fritos Chili Cheese, Doritos Cool Ranch, and Wavy Funyuns Onion.

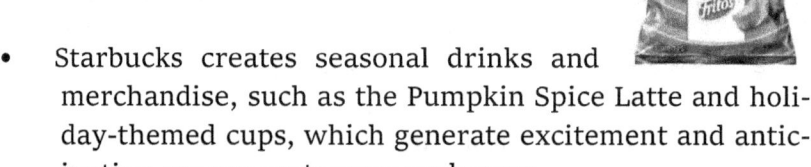

- Starbucks creates seasonal drinks and merchandise, such as the Pumpkin Spice Latte and holi-day-themed cups, which generate excitement and antic-ipation among customers each year.

Restaurants can offer a special dish at a specific time of year or day of the week. Similarly, a cleaning company might offer a 'spring-cleaning' package as winter recedes.

Retailers may make a product available only in-store and not online.

You can also use limited edition products to identify those that you could add to your standard range. These are often hailed as 'Back by popular demand'.

How to create a limited edition

1. Agree what goal a limited edition would serve, whether that's to create excitement, find long term new products, or increase revenue.

2. Brain-storm ideas for limited edition products.

3. Carry out consumer research to identify those products most likely to gain excitement or revenue.

4. Create memorable packaging that signifies 'limited edition', and stands out.

5. Launch the product with suitable promotional support.

ADOPT THE FREEMIUM MODEL

Freemium (free + premium) is a technique heavily used by SaaS (software as a service) companies to reduce the risk for customers by letting them try without cost. Autoresponder companies such as GetResponse do this, as does Spotify.

Many media businesses, such as the New York Times, also use the freemium model, by reducing the number of articles you can read for free. F2P (free to play) games often include micropayments, where gamers pay for extra items such as weapons.

The aim of freemium is to get people accustomed to using your product, Then, at a certain point, they hit a limitation, which encourages them to pay for the extra capacity, functionality, support or other resource.

Sometimes the consumer will see additional features that hadn't occurred to them when they first joined up. For example, Zapier's users will see new ways of using the service.

Using a freemium model, you can see what percentage of free users convert to the paid version, and change the model over time to maximize your revenue. The free version of Spotify, for example, restricts how many songs you have access to, and limits the number of skips you can make per hour.

Some free versions include advertisements, which generates revenue and causes irritation. This happens in mobile phone apps and YouTube. Light users may find these limitations acceptable, particularly if they aren't too intrusive.

The main drawback of freemium is the cost attributable to the freeloaders who use your service. Only 1% to 10% of users will ever pay a monthly fee. So your aim is to achieve an adequate conversion rate, and minimize the cost of the free subscribers.

It isn't easy to make freemium work, and some businesses pivot to free time-limited trials or simply stop providing a free product.

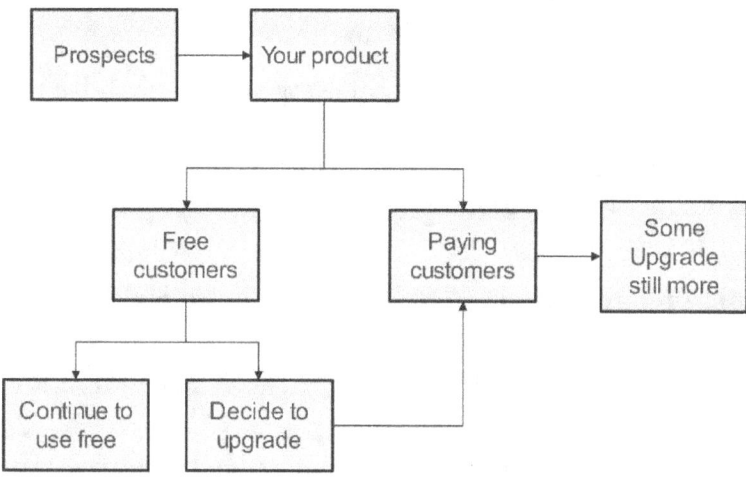

The Freemium model

How to add a freemium option

1. Determine whether your product would allow for a free tier. This will require a digital service where the marginal cost of extra users is minimal.

2. Develop a structure that would attract and convert the

maximum number of users. Be aware of the risks of can-nibalizing existing paid users.

3. Implement and monitor your freemium product.

COME OUT FIGHTING

You've a mainstream food brand that's suffering from cheap supermarket own brands. So, what do you do? The answer might be to create a fighting brand, one that matches the gro-cery store's price. That way, you scoop up price sensitive cus-tomers who would defect, and keep those who value your brand qualities.

In some cases, your fighting brand might be identical to its higher priced version, but with different packaging.

Businesses tend to launch fighting brands at three points:

1. At times of recession, when consumers trade down to cheaper options.

2. When a low price or no-frills competitor enters the mar-ket. The arrival of budget airlines is a case in point.

3. As a market matures and products become generic, such as happened in the PC market.

But there's a risk. The store might de-list your main brand, because it has limited space for your category. Alternatively, the fighting brand might cannibalize your premium brand, because consumers don't value the difference between the two.

Research suggests you must identify at least one unique must-have feature for the premium segment, and remove it from the fighter brand. That way, the risk of cannibalization is minimal. So, if cat food buyers value the scent of your premium brand, you could remove it from your fighting brand.

But do you have the time and money to focus on a new brand when you're already fighting on other fronts? And do you have the skills and mindset to produce and market a low-price brand?

Qantas managed to launch its low-price Jetstar airline to fight off Virgin Blue. But many full price airlines failed in their attempts to beat the budget carriers.

FIGHTING BRAND #2: OUT ON ITS OWN

As we saw previously, some observers regard a fighter brand as one that competes on price. But there is an alternative view about what constitutes a fighting brand.

This is one that's characterized by its strong and distinctive identity. It has a clear and consistent message that resonates with its target audience, and it's not afraid to take risks and push the boundaries in order to get noticed. It also communicates its message through various platforms such as social media, television, and print advertisements, and events to reach its target audiences.

Fighting brands are known for their competitive spirit. They're constantly seeking ways to outdo their rivals and to gain an edge in the marketplace. They are constantly innovating and experimenting with new marketing strategies and tactics in order to stay ahead of the curve.

Fighting brands also have a strong sense of purpose and mission, which drives their marketing efforts. They are not just focused on selling products or services, but they also have a deeper message or cause they're trying to promote. This purpose helps them to connect with your target audience on a deeper level and to create a sense of loyalty and commitment among customers.

Ben and Jerry's (which sold out to Unilever) used to have a strong ethical stance, and still supports causes such as Black Lives Matter. But it's not just social issues marketing (which carries its risks, because consumers are alert to brands' bandwagon behavior). Red Bull regularly gains headlines for its eye-catching stunts.

How to implement a fighting brand

1. Create a brand that is distinctively different from your existing products. This allows you some room to disavow its activities.

2. Create a separate management, one with its own budget, tasked with treating the product as a fighting brand. Ideally, it should be physically housed away from the main business.

3. Launch the brand. Be prepared to support it for the long term.

PRODUCTIZE YOUR SERVICE

Imagine your garden is looking tired – it's covered in weeds and moss. So you call in a professional gardener, who tells you they can work on it at a certain rate per hour. That leaves you with some doubts. You're unsure what they'll do, and how much it will cost you.

So you look at another business, Green Thumb. Its website tells you exactly what work they will do, and what you will pay for their Basic, Standard or Ultimate program. Among the optional programs are the Oasis Water Conserver, Scarification, and the Stress Beater.

As a result, you know exactly what you'll get, and how much

you'll pay, and so you hire them.

Green Thumb, like other businesses, has productized its service, turning it into a packaged, tangible product that can be sold to customers.

The process involves standardizing your service and pricing it accordingly.

Advantages of Productizing a Service

Increased sales: The prospect knows in advance what they will receive, so they're more likely to buy.

Scalable: By packaging your service into a product, you can more easily scale your operations to meet increased demand. With a standardized service, it becomes easier to replicate and deliver to multiple customers at once.

More control: Breaking the service down into individual steps allows you to have a standard operating procedure. This means employees can be taught what to do, leading to reduced variation. It can also speed the onboarding of new staff, and permit the development of a franchised business

Streamlined Delivery: Productizing a service helps streamline the delivery process. Customers can purchase the product online or in-store, and the business can provide standardized support and training materials. This makes it easier to maintain consistent quality and reduces the need for customization.

Improved Customer Satisfaction: By setting clear expectations around what the service entails, the value it provides, and the outcomes customers can expect, you get happier customers. This clarity can increase trust and reduce buyer's remorse.

Reduction in waste: Formalizing your method of work may

prevent unnecessary 'busy work' that adds no value to the client and increases your costs.

Reduction in costs: You will spend less time explaining your service to prospects, writing proposals, and even removing the need for initial meetings.

Steps to Productize a Service

Standardize the service: Standardize the service by creating a clear process or methodology that can be replicated across different customers. This should include a defined scope, timeline, and outcome. This can be done by process mapping.

Develop your pricing: Determine the appropriate price levels for the product. Consider the levels of service, time taken and resources needed to supply each one, and the value the customer receives. Consider also what your competition is charging.

Package the Service: Package your service into a tangible product you can sell to customers. This may include marketing materials, training materials, and support resources.

To learn more, try "The Business of Process Mapping", by Robert Damelio.

Next we look at pricing and how it affects revenue.

What steps can you take to increase either the profitability of your product, or the revenue per transaction?

The buyer is entitled to a bargain. The seller is entitled to a profit. So there is a fine margin in between where the price is right. I have found this to be true to this day whether dealing in paper hats, winter underwear or hotels.
- Conrad Hilton

6. PRICING AND REVENUE TACTICS

LEADER PRICING

Leader pricing, also known as loss-leader pricing, is a pricing tactic in which you offer a product at a price significantly lower than its usual market price.

Grocery stores offer loss-leader items such as cereal or milk at a low price to attract customers to the store.

DIY or hardware stores sometimes sell drills at or below cost. This is because the customers may buy accessories such as drill bits with the new tool. The accessories often have a bigger profit margin, and can be impulse buys.

For businesses, leader pricing can help to increase foot traffic and awareness. You can also use leader pricing to clear out excess inventory, making room for new products.

Loss-leader pricing can be particularly attractive to customers during economic downturns, when they are more likely to look for ways to save money.

But there are risks associated with leader pricing. If you consistently offer items at a loss, you may struggle to remain profitable. If you can't sustain the low prices, customers may become frustrated and lose trust in your business. Moreover, loss-leader pricing may lead to retaliation by competitors, leading to a downward price spiral.

ADD AN ENTRY-LEVEL BRAND

Introducing a low-cost Entry-Level Brand (ELB) can give you many benefits. It appeals to first-time users who are budget-conscious and seeking to test the market before making a larger investment. By offering a more affordable option, you can tap into this market segment, attract new customers and increase your market share.

ELB can also be used as a tool for market penetration. By offering an affordable product, you can enter new market segments and increase its brand visibility. This can help you gain a foothold in the market and eventually lead to increased sales and profits.

But there are potential risks associated with introducing an ELB. The low cost of the product may harm the prestige of the existing brand and lower its perceived value. This may also lead to cannibalization of sales, as customers who would have otherwise purchased a higher-end product opt for the more affordable ELB instead.

To mitigate these risks, you have to consider your target market and the positioning of your ELB. The product should be marketed as a value-oriented option, without compromising the quality and reliability of your existing brand.

Companies that have successfully introduced an ELB include Samsung with its Galaxy A series, and Apple with its iPhone SE. Both companies were able to tap into new market segments and attract new customers, without damaging the prestige of their existing brand.

How to introduce an entry-level brand

1. Decide what features or support you could remove from a

product, or raw materials whose cost you could reduce.

2. Assess the impact of that on the product's cost.

3. Evaluate whether launching such a product might add revenue, cannibalize sales or weaken your image.

4. Decide whether to launch an entry-level brand.

PREDATORY PRICING

If you're in a particularly aggressive frame of mind, you can cut your prices to such an extent that your competitors have to drop theirs too, which causes them to lose money, and either go bust or exit the market.

Alternatively, they fail to reduce their prices, their customers defect to you, and the competitor goes bust.

At this point, you have a monopoly and can raise your prices again. Or you can buy up the competitor from the receivers at a bargain price.

Where tech firms such as Google and Amazon have a near monopoly, some fear they're biding their time before hiking their prices. An Economist article, "The Problem with Profits," suggests that tech platforms such as Google and Facebook "might not be rent-extracting monopolies yet, but investors value them as if they will be one day."

So, predatory pricing is an unsavory tactic, and not without its risks. What if the competitors have deep pockets and can outlast you? If you start a price war, it's hard to forecast how it will end. It may also be illegal, and you may end up in court.

Rather than face a monopoly inquiry, it may be better to have a few weak competitors whose presence in the market 'demonstrate' it's a free market.

MARGINAL PRICING

Marginal pricing is particularly advantageous for companies that provide digital products or services, such as software, e-books, online courses, and streaming services.

This is because once you've created a digital product, there are no extra costs associated with producing and delivering it to a customer.

That means you can charge a price that covers your fixed costs and generates a profit, without having to worry about the cost of producing each additional unit.

So, you could develop a software program and sell it to thousands of customers without incurring any additional production costs. Once you've recouped your development and marketing costs, every extra dollar is pure profit.

Such companies would point out that they still have overheads that need to be paid for, such as server, support, development, and advertising costs. But there are almost no costs associated with each additional sale.

The low marginal costs associated with digital products also means you can experiment with different pricing strategies, such as dynamic pricing, subscription-based pricing, and freemium models. This flexibility allows you to test different pricing strategies and find the one that works best for your business and customers.

What this means: Once you have a digital product, you have a lot of flexibility in how you charge for it. And there are few costs involved in scaling it. So, you can take on free users with the hope of an upsell, because they cost you nothing.

OFFER A SUBSCRIPTION

TV, newspapers and magazines have long offered subscriptions. The customer commits to paying for several months, in return for a reduced price. And the media gets a longer-term customer, and avoids paying the middleman.

For software businesses, there is the added advantage: the cost of servicing the extra months is small. So overall, a subscription model gives you many advantages:

- **A Predictable Revenue**: By charging customers a recurring fee, you can better forecast your revenue and plan your operations accordingly.

- **Customer Loyalty**: Subscription pricing can help you build customer loyalty by providing more contact, content and value to them.

- **Upselling Opportunities**: You get the chance to upsell customers to higher tiers of service or to offer additional products or services.

- **Inertia**: Some customers fail to cancel, which gives you revenue from customers that don't require servicing.

- **Lower access fees**. Subscriptions allow the user to access the product at a lower ticket than if offered only the full price. Customers focus on the reduced monthly cost ($10) rather than the overall annual cost ($120).

But subscriptions are no longer limited to media and SaaS businesses:

Automotive: car companies now bundle the price of the car, roadside assistance, insurance, insurance and maintenance into a single monthly payment. This removes the need for buyers to deal with different suppliers, and makes the car price more manageable.

Video games: Xbox, PlayStation and Nintendo all offer subscriptions. According to The Gamer, subscribers spend four times the amount of time, three times the amount of money, and play two and a half times the number of games compared with non-subscription-based gamers.

Apps: Health apps such as HeadSpace and Sleep Cycle provide subscription models that unlock premium benefits.

But there are challenges. *Retention* is an issue for businesses that use a subscription model. Meal kit companies often find customers leave after three months. Here are some ways to reduce churn:

- **Renewal**: Offer customers more benefits or extra value when they renew.

- **Gamification.** Give the customer rewards. It can be something as simple as a progress bar, a badge, or an online treasure hunt.

- **Unlock more benefits as time goes by.** With each passing month or quarter, surprise the customer with freebies or increased value.

The ideal subscription model is one where your product is a must-have rather than a nice-to-have. In other words, the consumer should feel the need to keep using your product. That is where the car companies succeed, whereas meal kits are at risk.

It is also easier for the car companies to offer to replace the car at regular intervals, whereas the pay-once purchaser might be inclined to keep the vehicle.

How to gain more customers using subscriptions

1. **Identify whether you can amend your product to a sub-**

scription model. You may need to offer both types of purchase, at least initially, in case the consumer rejects the new model. You should also ensure that the cost of one or two years' payments is cheaper than an outright purchase.

You may recall how Microsoft moved from one-off purchases of Office to a subscription model. Nowadays, people assume that is the norm. And as long as the subscription fee is higher than the income from the traditional purchasing cycle, you will be earning more.

2. **Work out how you can provide a bundle**, which will provide added value to the customer while also disguising the actual price.

3. Offer a discount for **new subscribers**.

FREE SHIPPING

Do you ever find yourself adding a product to an online shopping cart, only to find the price has increased due to shipping or other costs?

Shipping costs are the biggest cause of shopping cart abandonment, as the chart below shows.

In such cases, free shipping is the way to go. Customers are more likely to complete their purchase when they know you won't charge them for shipping, and this reduces shopping cart abandonment.

Free shipping improves customer satisfaction. Customers appreciate not having to pay for shipping, and this can lead to increased customer loyalty. It also reduces the friction involved when someone buys several items and gets unsure about what the final shipping costs will be.

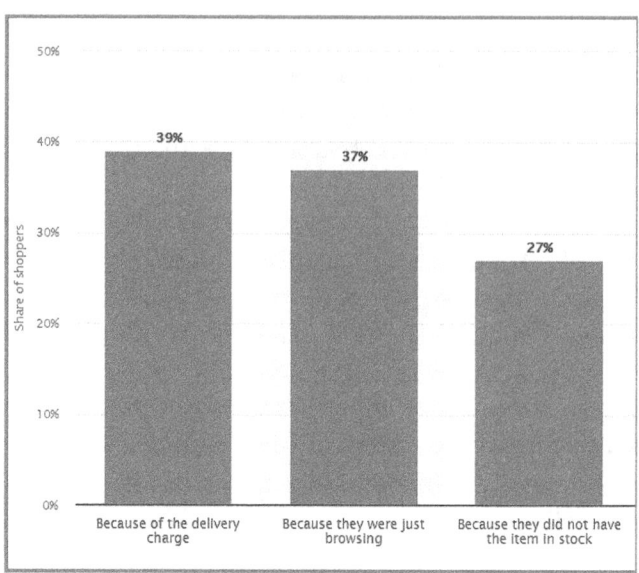

Shipping costs trouble consumers

CREATE AN ORDER THRESHOLD

"Threshold for what?" you may ask. The answer is, "It's the threshold where customer benefits start".

In other words, you notify the customer they'll get a benefit such as free delivery if their basket reaches a specific amount. This incentivizes them to buy more.

It makes sense because free shipping costs you money. So there's no point in giving them to customers who are buying very little from you.

And customers may choose to increase their spend to reach the threshold, especially if they see a cross-sell. So, setting a threshold serves to prevent unnecessary cost and encourages customers to increase their basket value.

To set up a threshold, you need to know your average order value (AOV). The shopping card business Shopify says it should be for the *mode* of your orders; that is, the *most frequently purchased* basket. You then set the benefit at, say, 30% above your AOV, and notify the customer on the website with a promotional banner announcing the benefit and the order threshold.

Few businesses provide free shipping on small orders. Amazon, for example, does that only for Prime customers. Hence, if you're offering free shipping, something that shoppers like, you only do it for sufficiently large orders.

Alternatively, some retailers provide a gift or discount when the threshold is reached.

But free shipping is a good incentive for all customers big and small. And you probably don't want to lose customers who are only making small purchases, by telling them that you will add a delivery charge, which is why inexpensive items often cost substantially more online than in a local shop, because the cost of delivery has been added into a delivery-inclusive price.

Yieldify says a campaign it ran for M&S France brought a 13:1 ROI and over 3,000 new leads.

Free shipping threshold, by Yunnan Sourcing

BUY NOW, PAY LATER

A study by research company Forrester showed that businesses using financing achieve at least 30% more sales than those that don't.

Allowing customers to pay by installments can increase your sales for several reasons:

- Increased Affordability: you give customers who can't afford to pay the full price upfront the option to pay in smaller amounts over time, making the purchase more affordable and accessible to more prospects.

- More Trust: Allowing customers to pay in installments may increase their trust in the company, as they can test the product or service before committing to the full amount.

- Increased Customer Loyalty: By offering flexible payment options, customers are more likely to make repeat purchases, leading to increased customer loyalty.

- Less Competition: Allowing customers to pay by installments can also give a company a competitive advantage over others who do not offer this option.

But there are risks, notably because people who can't readily afford your product may default on their payments. They may also be more likely to return the product.

And there is an ethical risk if you encourage people to spend money than they have and get into debt; so this needs to be managed carefully. You can seek to manage each customer's default, or their request for more time to pay, on an individual basis.

But overall, if you're selling high-priced items, some form of credit is essential.

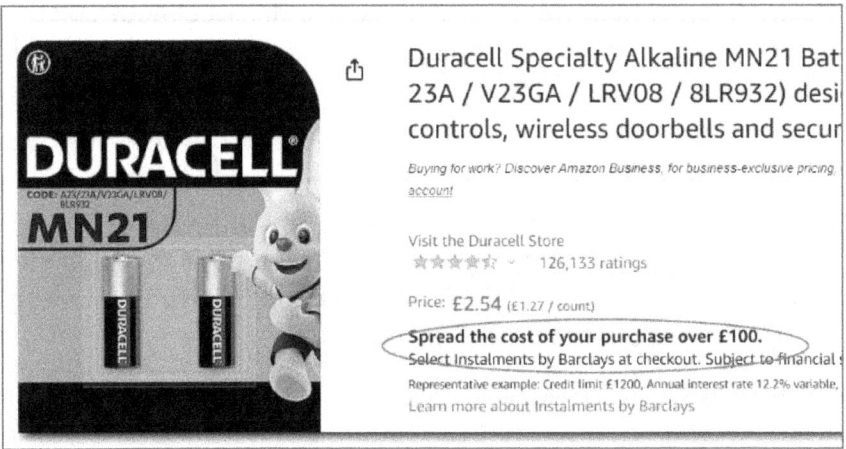

Don't offer installments for low-priced items!

FREE TRIAL

Offering a free trial gives potential customers a risk-free opportunity to experience your product or service before committing to a purchase. When they're able to try your product or service without paying, they're more likely to buy it.

In the software industry, many companies offer a 30—day free trial of their software. This gives prospects the opportunity to test drive the software, see if it meets their needs, and experience the full functionality before committing to a purchase.

Such companies usually take a customer's credit card details, and payment automatically starts 30 days later. It's a form of 'inertia selling', because some customers simply forget to cancel. But this can lead to complaints. Recognizing this, some businesses don't request a credit card until the 30-day period expires. This causes more friction in the marketing process, because the customer has to take action when the impulse to buy has faded.

A free trial is sometimes called a 'puppy dog sale'. A pet shop may let you take the puppy home for the weekend, and see how you like it. Most people will decide to keep it, not least because the kids won't let you take it back. The same applies to car companies that let you drive a car for several days.

The risk is that people will use your product, never intending to keep it. So you end up with second-hand goods. You can avoid this by qualifying people and excluding the high-risk ones. That in turn risks alienating people who fully intend to buy your product but are rejected.

But overall, a free trial is a win-win situation for both the business and the customer. The business benefits from increased sales and the customer benefits from a risk-free opportunity to experience the product or service.

COMPLEMENTARY PRODUCT PRICING

You may be dazzled by the bargain price of a printer, only to find that the ink cartridges cost a fortune.

Many people are now aware of that trick, and wise business buyers focus on the total cost of ownership (TCO).

But there is scope for complementary product pricing in other markets, so it's worth considering whether you can tie consumables into your main product.

This device is commonly used by businesses whose products require accessories, consumables, or services to function properly.

Complementary product pricing can help you maintain your profit margins by reducing the severity of price competition.

By charging less for your main product, and more for consumables, you can protect your overall profit margin when competitors offer lower prices on your main products. This can be particularly beneficial if you're selling expensive products, as it allows you to reduce their price.

And it can help you generate additional revenue from the sale of complementary products.

The risk is that customer will have the best of both worlds. They'll buy your main product cheaply and then buy lookalike accessories. If you try to make your add-ons a requirement, you may fall foul of legislation.

Typical examples of complementary product pricing include the following:

Razor and blades: A classic example of complementary product pricing is the razor and blade model, where a company sells razors at a low price and then charges premium prices for replacement blades.

Printers and ink cartridges: We've seen this is a common strategy in this market.

Gaming consoles and games: Gaming console manufacturers often sell their consoles at a low price and then charge a lot for the video games.

Electric shavers and replacement heads: Electric shaver businesses typically sell the main product at a low price and then charge a premium price for replacement heads, which are necessary for the shavers to function effectively.

Fitness equipment and workout accessories: Companies that sell fitness equipment often sell the main product at a low price and then charge premium prices for workout accessories, such as weights, resistance bands, and other complementary products that enhance the functionality of the main product.

AUTOSHIP

With autoship, you regularly deliver products to your customers on a scheduled basis, without requiring any additional action from the customer.

This is done through a subscription model, where your customer signs up for the program and chooses how often they would like to receive the product.

You charge the customer at regular intervals and their selected product is automatically shipped to them. This eliminates the need for the customer to remember to place an order or reorder the product, which saves time and ensures they never run out of the product they need.

Autoship programs offer the business several benefits. It provides a reliable and recurring revenue stream, as customers are committed to continuing their subscription.

It reduces the workload for customer service and sales teams, as the process of ordering and shipping is automated. And thirdly, it builds customer loyalty, as customers are more likely to continue using the product if they receive it regularly.

Dollar Shave Club, which offers men's grooming products, has a successful autoship program. Another example is Birchbox, which offers a monthly subscription box for beauty and skincare products.

55% of retail subscriptions are for curated bundles. It's for the consumer who wants a surprise and variety. You open your box and find several small items to try out. Most of the remaining market goes to replenishment products. In this case, you're getting your essential supplies shipped automatically at a set frequency. That might include toilet paper, meal kits or dog food.

CULL YOUR LOW SELLERS

The 80/20 rule, also known as the Pareto Principle, suggests that 80% of your sales come from 20% of your products. You can apply this principle to your product line as well, meaning that a small portion of your products will usually produce the majority of your revenue.

As a result, it's crucial to focus your attention and resources on your top-selling products.

That allows you to optimize your production and marketing efforts to increase sales and profitability. Doing that can improve your product's quality, reduce its costs, or create more effective marketing campaigns. Additionally, you can use customer feedback from your top-selling products to inform product development for the future.

Meanwhile, culling low sellers has additional advantages. It allows you to redirect your resources and focus on products that are more likely to drive revenue. Secondly, it can help you streamline your operations by reducing the number of products you need to manage and stock. This, in turn, can help reduce costs and increase efficiency.

How to implement the Pareto Principle

1. Analyze which products produce the majority of profit.

2. Consider the benefits and risks of culling the remainder of your products.

3. Decide what steps you should take to optimize your costs and revenues.

4. Consider applying the Pareto Principle to other parts of the business, such as advertising, depots, and staffing.

Procter & Gamble cut 100 brands from its line-up, to focus on its big sellers like Tide. The company aimed to improve its financial performance by focusing on the 80 brands that generate 95 percent of its profits and 90 percent of sales. P&G also wanted to ensure that its products had a strategic fit, which meant selling off brands such as the Braun small electronic appliances.

ANCHOR YOUR PRICE

You're in a store, looking at a coffee machine. The price label says ~~$240~~ $190. Wow, you're going to save $50 on the coffee machine! That's the anchoring effect. Maybe the machine is only worth $150, but your brain sees only the anchor value.

The next day, you're in a car dealer's showroom. The car is priced at $20,000, and the salesman whispers that he could probably do it for $18,000. Bargain! But once again, that's the anchor effect. The dealer only ever expects to sell that vehicle for $18,000.

And finally, you're in a restaurant, inspecting the wine menu. You notice one bottle of wine at $70, some bottles at $18, and a few priced around $25. You decide to buy a $25 bottle of wine. And the waiter thinks, 'You, I knew you'd buy that. Not too cheap, and not too expensive"

Does the restaurant ever sell the $70 bottle of wine? Rarely, if at all. The pricey wine is only there to anchor the prices.

Grocers frequently use anchoring in their multi-pack offers. In the offer below, you could buy not 12 but 36 bottles of beer (3 packs of 12), by spending just that bit more money. Do you really want that much beer? But, hey, it's on offer.

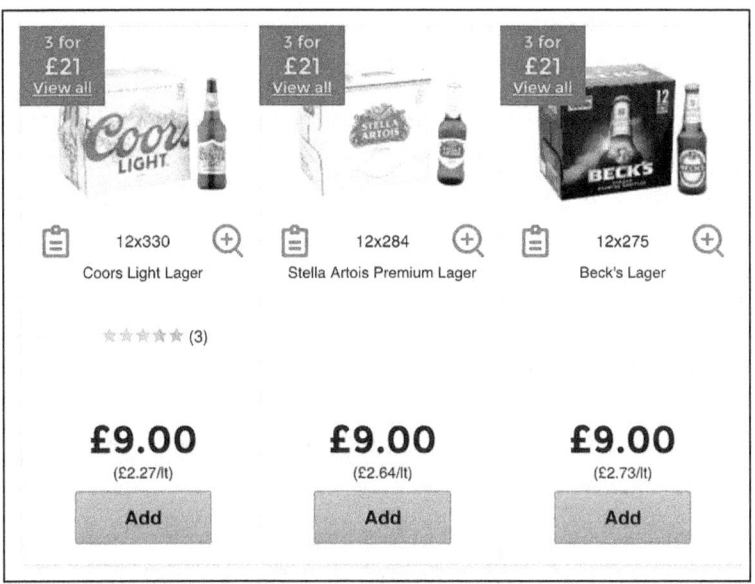

3 for £21 View all	3 for £21 View all	3 for £21 View all
12x330	12x284	12x275
Coors Light Lager	Stella Artois Premium Lager	Beck's Lager
★★★★★ (3)		
£9.00	**£9.00**	**£9.00**
(£2.27/lt)	(£2.64/lt)	(£2.73/lt)
Add	Add	Add

36 bottles are cheaper per bottle than 12, but may affect your waistline.

How to implement your price anchor

1. Work out how you can anchor the price of your product lines to make the main brand look good value. This might involve adding a cheaper or more expensive product.

2. Sell multi-packs that increase the value of the shopping basket.

3. Offering a product with a reduced-price sticker (allowing for legal requirement) you can make your product look good value.

SHRINKFLATION

If you're seeking to reduce your costs, "shrinkflation" is one way to achieve that. You reduce the size of your pack or portion, while keeping the price the same.

The Cocoa Puffs' family size box fell from 19.3 ounces to 18.1 ounces, while Cinnamon Toast Crunch dropped from 19.3 ounces to 18.8 ounces. The new, smaller boxes were priced the same as the previous ones, so consumers lost a bowl of cereal with the new box, but they were saved a price increase.

By reducing the quantity of the product, you save on raw material costs, production costs and transportation. This helps you maintain or boost profitability while avoiding any increase in the price of the product, which could reduce demand.

Shrinkflation is particularly effective when you're facing rising costs, whether for raw materials, energy or labor.

But there are risks associated with shrinkflation. Prime among them is getting negative feedback on social media.

Consumers often feel cheated when they notice a reduction in the size of a product. This can lead to negative reviews, reduced customer loyalty, and ultimately a decline in sales.

Another risk is that your customers may switch to cheaper brands. This risk is particularly significant in price-sensitive categories. This applies to products that people purchase frequently, such as household essentials. The customer may perceive they are not getting as much value for their money and may switch to cheaper alternatives.

Categories that have the most to gain from shrinkflation are those where brand name is crucial in driving consumer behavior. Luxury brands or premium products that are perceived to be of higher quality may be able to reduce the product's size, without losing sales.

On the other hand, categories where price and quantity are important are more likely to lose customers if they adopt a shrinkflation strategy.

How to reduce the impact of shrinkflation or disguise it

1. Keep the reduction small. Consumers are less likely to notice a reduction of under 10%.

2. Change the pack at the same time. Dawn soap introduced a more convenient squeezy bottle that opened from the bottom, while reducing the contents from 19fl oz to 15 fl oz. Or, do what Pedigree Dentastix did, and introduce a new pack design.

3. Suggest that the smaller pack is more convenient, if there is evidence that the existing pack is too large, A carpet tile company reduced its pack size from 20 to 15 tiles, on the genuine grounds that the box was too heavy for the carpet fitters.

4. Point out that the new pack reduces waste, if customers were not consuming all the product in the larger size.

5. Keep the container the same size.

Next, we examine tactics that ease your customer's journey.

Psychology plays a big role in marketing. So, in the next chapter we look at tactics such as improving the customer's mood or winning their loyalty.

We start with friction – the things that get in the way of a successful purchase.

A satisfied customer is the best business strategy of all.
- Michael LeBoeuf

7. CUSTOMER TACTICS

TALK TO YOUR CUSTOMERS

Remarkably few businesses talk to their customers. This means most are unaware of their concerns, hopes and fears.

In one case, a contractor said they avoided buying products from one floor tile company because the boxes were too heavy to carry. The answer was to reduce the number of floor tiles per box. Yet the company's management hadn't known about this longstanding problem because they'd never spent time with their customers.

Sales people often have vital information which is never passed upwards, either because they see it as "just the way it is", or because there's no culture of exchanging information. Spend time with a top salesperson, and you'll learn a lot.

Alternatively, phone or visit customers, and ask their advice. Once they know you aren't trying to sell them something, they'll relax. Do this in an informal environment, either in a bar or by taking them out to lunch, and they'll give you their thoughts freely.

REMOVE THE FRICTION

How many of your prospects abandon their shopping basket on your ecommerce site, or leave your bricks and mortar store because they can't find what they're looking for?

Friction is any obstacle or inconvenience that prevents someone from becoming a customer. Common sources of friction include complex purchasing processes, unclear pricing, poor website usability, slow loading times, and lack of trust.

The next time you're in a restaurant, see how long you have to wait at the entrance before being greeted, let alone being seated? How long does it take to have your order taken, how long to catch a waiter's eye to ask for the check, or to queue at a checkout?

It's also useful to identify and track key metrics such as conversion rates, bounce rates, and cart abandonment rates, as these can be indicators of friction points.

To overcome friction, you need to simplify the purchasing process, make pricing and product information clear and easily accessible, improve your website performance, and build trust with customers through transparent practices and positive customer experiences.

How to identify and remove friction

1. Carry out research:

2. Perform user testing

3. Undertake customer research

4. Analyze website analytics

5. Collect customer feedback

6. Analyze the findings, and summarize the main friction issues.

7. Implement solutions to resolve them.

IMPULSIVE CUSTOMERS

The lower the product price, the most it's likely to be an impulse purchase. We happily pick up a chocolate bar when waiting in a supermarket queue. And even in the most traditional of markets, you can foster spontaneous purchase. Americans spend $276 on impulse purchases every month. Top purchases are toys, clothing, groceries and clothing.

Some of the ways that businesses generate impulse buys are:

• Limited time promotions, thus creating urgency

• An attractive in-store display

• Showing complementary products at the checkout

Fast food chains like McDonald's often use signage and advertising to promote limited time menu items, creating a sense of urgency for customers to try the item before it's gone. Convenience stores like 7-Eleven also place candy and snacks near the cash register, capitalizing on the impulsive nature of customers who are already in a buying mood.

Another way you make your products and services impulse buys is by creating an attractive in-store display. Retailers like Sephora often place high-end beauty products at eye level and display them in a visually appealing manner, making them more enticing for customers to purchase.

Additionally, you can also make your products and services impulse buys by providing a seamless purchasing experience. Online retailers like Amazon make it easy for customers to add items to their cart and check out quickly, reducing the time and effort it takes to make a purchase.

How to boost impulse purchasing

1. Make people feel they're getting a deal.

2. In a bricks and mortar outlet, provide background music, strategically placed point of purchase displays, and tempting window displays. Train checkout assistants to suggest an upsell.

3. Use the store layout to guide shoppers past impulse buys.

4. Show complementary items next to higher priced goods.

5. Provide optional top-up items.

6. Use vouchers, free sampling demonstrations, videos and conditional promotions (such as BOGOF deals).

7. Emphasize seasonal items.

MAKE IT PLAYFUL

By playful, we don't mean jokey or lightweight. It's about encouraging customers to engage more with you. And that's where the principle of gamification comes in.

Gamification refers to the use of game design strategies to engage and motivate people to take specific actions.

Domino's Pizza increased its sales revenue by 30%, through its Pizza Hero game. It lets customers customize their pizza in a game-like environment by dropping toppings onto the pizza. The user then has the option to order their personal pizza.

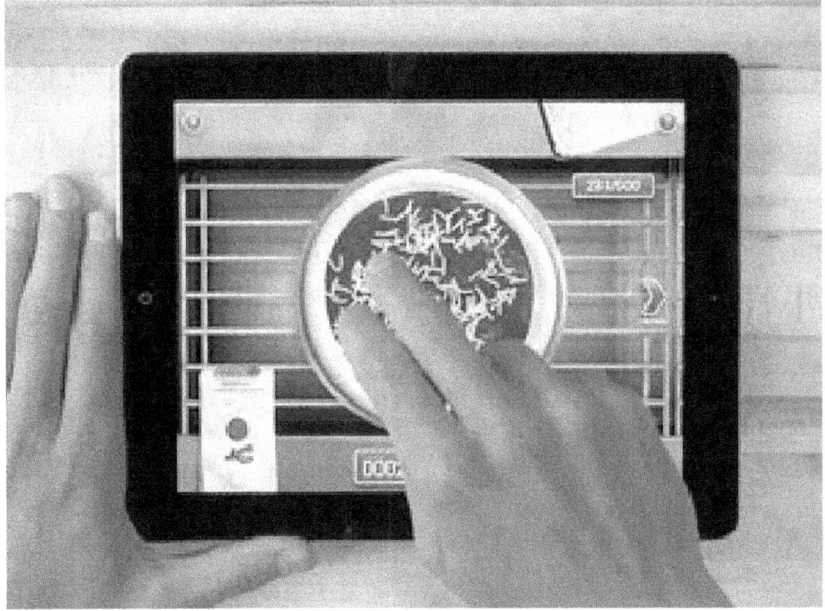

The Pizza Hero game

By rewarding customers, and incorporating an element of competition or play into the customer journey, you create an interactive experience.

For example, a clothing retailer could create a quiz for customers to find their personal style and then offer discounts on products that fit their style. This provides value to the customer, but also increases the chances of them making a purchase.

Another example is using leaderboards in a loyalty program. Customers can earn points for making purchases, writing reviews, or referring friends. These points can then be redeemed for rewards or used to rank customers on a leaderboard, adding a competitive aspect to the program and encouraging customers to engage more with the brand.

Gamification can also improve customer retention. A mobile app could include a rewards program that encourages customers to make repeat purchases and engage with the brand regularly. The app could include mini-games that provide a fun and engaging experience while also reinforcing the brand's messaging.

Other advantages provided by gamification include acquiring customer details, educating the customer about your products and reviving lapsed purchasers.

How to introduce gamification

1. Identify the key points along a customer's journey, including the first time they make contact. Consider whether you could provide a reward in any of those steps.

2. Through research, understand the kinds of social media your customers like to engage with. Do those channels provide gamification?

3. See whether competitors or comparator businesses include gamification, and whether you could adopt those principles.

4. From what you have learnt, trial some element of reward, play or competition into your messaging.

MOVING PEOPLE UP THE LOYALTY LADDER

How loyal are your customers? Would they defect to a competitor if offered slightly lower prices? Or would they always stick by you, and even tell others what great products you have?

Amazon, Apple, Netflix, and Domino's Pizza are among the

enviable companies that have the most loyal customers.

A marketing ladder represents the different stages your customer goes through in their journey with your brand. The ladder is usually comprised of four or five rungs, each representing a different level of customer engagement and loyalty.

On the bottom rung are the Suspects, people who are aware of your products or services, but haven't yet bought them. Above those are Trialists, people who have used your product for the first time.

The middle rungs consist of the Customers. These are people who have made a purchase and are starting to develop an opinion about your company.

And on the top rungs are the Supports and Advocates, those who are highly engaged and loyal to your brand.

To move customers up the ladder, you need to create a positive experience at each stage. This may involve the following:

- Use marketing to get people to try your product.

- Provide quality products and services

- Offer helpful customer service

- Maintain communications with your customers

- Create a two-way dialogue with customers

- Drive engagement.

If you were a clothing retailer, you might start by using social media and influencer partnerships to build awareness of your stores.

As customers make their first purchase, you may provide

them with a personalized shopping experience, along with information about your rewards program.

By consistently offering high-quality stock and excellent customer service, you build loyalty and encourage repeat purchases. And over time, you offer exclusive events, promotions, and other incentives to keep your most engaged customers coming back.

A **loyalty program** may offer money-back deals for regular or high spending customers. Some grocery stores give customers who check in with a loyalty card give them points according to their spend, sometimes around 1% or 2% of their spend.

This means the benefits are invisible to casual shoppers. Other stores give a reduction on items that the loyal shopper buys regularly.

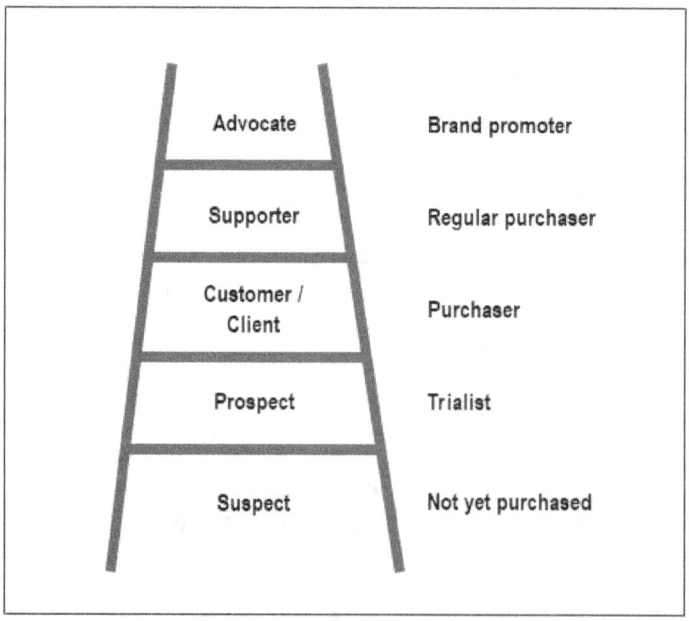

The loyalty ladder

GET THEM HOOKED

To get regular purchases, you can make your product or service habit-forming by designing it to address people's psychological needs, such as the need for social validation, control and consistency.

You can do that through features such as gamification, social integration, reward structures, and feedback mechanisms that tap into users' emotions and motivations.

The advantages are numerous. When customers develop a habit of using your product or service, they're more likely to continue using it regularly, which leads to increased engagement, loyalty and customer lifetime value.

Facebook and other platforms have habit-forming characteristics. They tap into our need for social validation and connection. The "like" button and the ability to post and receive updates from friends creates a reward structure that keeps users coming back to the platform to see if they have received any new notifications.

Unfortunately, habit-forming only works for products or services that are bought regularly, and where the purchase brings some special pleasure. This rules out most categories, such as homewares, cars and holidays.

Convenience goods: toilet paper, shampoo or milk. Also known as fast-moving consumer goods (FMCG), these are the necessities that we buy regularly. We get them from the grocery store. Most people buy the same brand without thinking. To that extent, they are hooked on those products. But unless you're offering something unique, it may not take much for the customer to defect.

Durables: They are items that are designed to last. They include low-cost items such as clothes, as well as more expensive items such as bicycles, cars and vacations.

Some durables come into the sub-category of **Speciality goods**, those that have a special identity and command a price premium, such as specific brands of luxury cars, photographic equipment, audio equipment, perfumes and high-fashion clothing, or even beer from niche breweries.

Veblen goods are those that defy the laws of economics: their sales increase as their price grows. These products have a cachet that denotes style, exclusivity or affluence. Examples might be Rolex watches or a Lamborghini car. If you want to know the price, you probably can't afford it.

Unsought goods include fire extinguishers, batteries, and life insurance. We buy them because the old one needs replacing, or because we fear what would happen if we lacked it. These are often grudge purchases, things we buy because we have to, such as tires. But if you're a motorcyclist, you will probably read reviews of tires, because they're what keep you safe. Hence, for a biker, the tire may be a speciality good.

Business products: bricks, earth coming equipment, crane hire and office leasing. Some people further classify them into more detailed sub-categories, such as high-priced capital goods versus accessories, which might include sandpaper. There isn't much opportunity to hook customers in this category.

Services. Here we tend to think of apps and online platforms such as Fitbit and Etsy, TikTok and WhatsApp. But many services also provide products. They include cafés, bars, restaurants and grocery stores. Because they get regular visits, retailers have a bigger scope for getting their customers hooked, with loyalty cards or personalized promotions.

IMPROVE YOUR CUSTOMER SERVICE

We have all read reviews of bad customer service in a newspaper or on Trustpilot. Yet, according to Forbes, companies that lead in customer experience outperform laggards by nearly 80%, and American consumers will pay 17% more to purchase from a company with a reputation for great service.

It is self-evident that bad customer experience adversely affects sales as it leads to unhappy customers who are less likely to return and will tell others about their negative experience. This can lead to a decrease in brand reputation and ultimately, a decline in sales.

Improving customer experience does the reverse, with positive word-of-mouth referrals and online reviews creating more sales. Some ways to improve customer experience include:

- **Personalization** - providing customers with a customized experience that meets their individual needs.

- **Communication** - ensuring clear and prompt communication with customers to address any concerns or questions they may have.

- **Empathy** - putting yourself in the customer's shoes to understand their needs and provide appropriate solutions.

- **Convenience** - making it easy for customers to interact with a business, whether through online or in-person channels.

- **Follow-up** - following up with customers to ensure their needs have been met and to ask for feedback on their experience.

LOCK IN YOUR CUSTOMERS

The last thing you want is for customers to defect to one of your competitors. You can try all you can to foster customer loyalty, but even the most loyal of customers can be fickle.

One solution is to create lock-in. Here are some ways to do that.

Unique products and services: You should seek to provide a unique value proposition that customers can't find elsewhere. That makes it hard for customers to switch. Personalizing products or services is one way to do that.

Increase the cost and difficulty of moving: You can also make it difficult and costly for customers to switch. You could make it difficult to transfer data or information from one platform to another, or charge high fees for doing so. This will discourage customers from switching and make them more likely to stay with you.

Build a network: Another strategy is to use a network effect, where you encourage customers to invite their friends, family, and colleagues to join the platform. The more people join your platform, the more valuable it becomes to everyone, making it less likely for customers to leave.

Brand image: Another way to create digital lock-in is by creating a brand that customers trust and identify with. This way, customers are less likely to switch to a different platform, even if it offers similar features and services.

Next we examine tactics for communicating with the customer.

In the next chapter we look at *information*, where we aren't trying to sell, just providing prospects with the information they need as a prelude to them buying from us.

And we also cover the more *promotional* aspects of communication. Let's start with the subject of "touchpoints".

The two words 'information' and 'communication' are often used interchangeably, but they signify quite different things. Information is giving out; communication is getting through.
- Sydney J. Harris

8. COMMUNICATION TACTICS

THE 7 TOUCHPOINTS

It's said that the customer needs to connect with you seven times before buying.

They might see your ad, encounter a social media post, hear a friend mention it, pass your stand at an industry event, or see your logo. These are all touch points.

They might not see all of these things, and they may see some of them more than once. But the principle is that *few people will buy your product the first time they see it.*

A business was changing its accountant recently. They asked people in their local area Facebook group for advice, and two or three names were mentioned. The company looked at their websites, checked them out on Google, and emailed a couple. Then they spoke to one on the phone. This was followed by another, more detailed email exchange. All of these were touchpoints. And finally, they made a decision.

The number and nature of touchpoints depends on how spontaneous the purchase is. If on a sunny day at the seaside you decide to buy an ice cream, you won't spend time interviewing the ice cream seller.

That said, you might have passed several vendors, noticed bright ice cream flags on shops, and seen other people enjoying an ice cream, all of which suggested you really should stop and buy one.

The 7 Touchpoints principle should remind us of the importance of small but important touchpoints. Do you send a 'thank you' email after a meeting? Do you give away pens with your logo on them?

We should also be aware of the risk of spreading our activity too widely. You can't be active on *every* social media platform. Sometimes it's best to concentrate your resources. But at its heart, the 7 Touchpoints tells us there are many places a consumer goes to, some of which we may be unaware of; and we ignore them at our peril.

Google's view

Google's research suggested an extension of this idea, the 7-11-4 rule. This says the consumer will spend 7 hours researching your product, reading reviews, comparing the competition and consuming content about your brand. They will do that across 11 touch points and in 4 different locations before they're ready to buy.

The locations could be online and offline, including your website, an in-person discussion, and a poster. But this seems very specific to search marketing and the world of Google.

Imagine you're thinking about where to go on holiday. Your decision will result from your experiences over many years, weekends spent chatting with your partner, and the two of you spending hours looking at hotels online. It's certainly not a decision that you'd make in seven hours.

How to implement the 7 Touchpoints

1. Identify the people and places your prospect might encounter during a purchasing decision.

2. Create content suitable for each non-human touchpoint.

3. Train your human contacts – not just sales people, but the receptionist and delivery drivers too, how to be the best possible ambassadors.

4. Allocate resources that will ensure your name becomes visible in those places.

MEANINGLESS DISTINCTIVENESS IS OK

Created by Byron Sharp in his book How Brands Grow, "Meaningless distinctiveness and glittering generalities" are tactics you can use to differentiate your business from your competitors.

Meaningless distinctiveness refers to creating an image of uniqueness or superiority through seemingly insignificant or superficial differences. It is the opposite of a meaningful claim. A restaurant that boasts about having unique ketchup dispensers or offering a special seasoning blend can create a sense of distinction, even if it does not have any real impact on the food itself.

Glittering generalities, on the other hand, refers to vague or abstract words that evoke positive emotions without specifying what the product or service actually offers. For instance, you might claim to offer "the best quality" without explaining what makes your product superior to others.

By creating a point of difference, you can distinguish your business from your competitors and create a perception of superiority. This, in turn, can help attract customers who are looking for something special or unique.

However, these tactics should not be used at the expense of providing a real USP and actual value to customers. Ideally, you should focus on providing real value to ensure these tactics do not backfire, with the risk of you becoming an object of ridicule.

Sharp, however, was not focused on rational claims, ones that could be measured. He said marketers should focus on making their brands attractive and memorable through a range of sensory and semantic branding cues such as colors, logos, tag lines, symbols and characters, celebrities and advertising styles. This might include the Nike swoosh, the Adidas three-stripe logo, and UPS's brown livery.

And Sharp might have appreciated the sheep dog that for 60 years has featured in Dulux paint tins and its marketing materials. According to legend, the dog belonged to the advertising director responsible for the company's 1961 campaign. It kept invading the set to play with the child actors, and was so adorable they decided to feature him.

THE POWER OF CASE STUDIES

Imagine you're an architect who's drawing up plans for a new house. You're a bit anxious about the specifications your picky client wants. So you start to flick through websites, trying to absorb the knowledge.

Then you come to a supplier's site which has case studies that discuss the same problem that you're experiencing. You feel reassured. The case studies show how a similar architect with a similar need has achieved the result you need. So you pick up the phone and ask for a consultation.

Case studies are detailed accounts of specific projects, products, or services that a company has provided to its customers. They're a powerful marketing tool because they demonstrate how the company has helped real customers solve real problems, which builds trust and credibility.

To create a successful case study, you identify a customer who has achieved a significant outcome as a result of using your products or services. You then conduct an in-depth interview with them to understand the challenges they faced, the solution they implemented, and the results they achieved.

You can use this information to create a story that highlights your unique value, and demonstrates your expertise and experience in solving similar problems.

You can then use this and other case studies in sales presentations or in email campaigns, or share them on social media to reach a wider audience.

HubSpot, an inbound marketing and sales business, uses case studies to show how its customers have used the platform to drive real business results, such as increased leads, conversions and revenue.

AIRSTREAM

Airstream Generates 78% More Leads at Scale with HubSpot

As Airstream grew, they needed a simple way to generate more leads at scale and distribute them amongst their network of dealers. Here's how Airstream increased lead generation and aligned marketing efforts with HubSpot.

HubSpot case study.

HOW TO MAKE PAID ADS PAY

With pay-per-click (PPC) advertising, you only pay when someone clicks on your online ad. This happens when Google, which has 80% of the PPC market, shows your ad. In turn, this happens when a keyword you've listed matches the visitor's question.

So, if you're selling overalls, and you've added that word to your list, and someone types in 'heavy-duty overalls' into Google, your ad will show up. But you only pay if the visitor then clicks on your ad.

With PPC, there's no wastage. You'll quickly discover exactly which keywords work for you, and you can add negative keywords. In the example above, you might add 'children' as a negative word, so people looking for kids' clothes won't see your ad.

You can also limit your ads to specific regions or cities, demographics, languages and times. This means you can use PPC to launch a new product or drive sales during the holiday season. If you have a local audience, you can reach customers looking for a specific service in your area, such as a plumbing or electrical work. And a B2B company can target decision-makers without wasting money.

You can set your budget, so you won't spend more than you're comfortable with. But be aware that Google (and Bing, which has the remainder of the PPC market) will encourage you to spend more.

They prefer to manage your spend, claiming their algorithm knows more than you ever could, and will create better results. That hasn't been everyone's experience. You may find that Google increases the cost of each click, which means your budget is quickly spent, and so you reach fewer people. So much for their clever algorithm.

The marketing gurus tend to like Facebook ads, which is odd.

Facebook's targeting is sloppy - because you can't accurately identify who wants to buy your product. Facebook ads are traditional 'interruption marketing'. You break into people's conversations.

WIN WITH SOCIAL MEDIA

Whenever people have a spare moment, out comes their phone. You only have to sit on a train, wait in a queue, or be in a café to see people thumbing their way down lines of social media posts.

And that's the allure of social media for any business. You get in among people as they read and post. Here are some of the main reasons why you would engage in social media marketing.

- **Increase your brand awareness**: Social media allows you to reach a wider audience and increase their visibility. By posting regularly, you can create a strong brand presence and attract new customers.

- **Communicate directly with customers**: The social media platforms let you respond to inquiries, provide customer support, and build a relationship with your audience.

- **Cost-effective**: Posting on social media is free, in so far as you only pay your staff. This makes it an affordable option for small businesses with limited budgets.

- **Increased website traffic**: Providing links to your website can drive traffic to the site and increase the chances of conversions.

How to implement a social media campaign

1. **Define your target audience**: It's important to understand who your target audience is, what social media platforms they use, and what type of content they engage with. There is, for example, a big difference in the needs of a local café and, say, a global accountancy practice.

2. **Create a content strategy**: This should speak to your target audience. There might be a mix of informative, educational, and entertaining content, as well as promotions.

3. **Engage with your audience**: Respond to comments and messages in a timely manner and interact with your followers.

4. **Use visuals**: Visual content, such as images and videos, usually perform better on social media than text-based content.

5. **Use influencers**: Partnering with influencers who have a strong following in your target market can help you reach a wider audience and build credibility for your brand.

6. **Track your results**: Use analytics tools to track your social media performance and measure the impact of your efforts. This will help you refine your strategy and make data-driven decisions.

ADD MORE CONTENT

Google loves content. It uses it as a measure of how useful your site is. So, the more content you put on your site, the better your ranking will be. But content is also there to help your customers, and solve their problems and demonstrate trustworthiness.

There are several types of content you can include on your website to engage and inform your target audience.

- **Blog Posts**: This type of content provides valuable information to the audience and helps establish the business as an industry leader. Blog posts can cover topics related to the business' products, services, or industry news. A fashion brand can write blog posts on the latest fashion trends, while a tech company can discuss new technology advances. If the word 'blog post' is off-putting, think of it as simply 'articles' that help your customers.

- **Product Pages**: Give your visitors enough content about your product or service. This might include features, specifications and benefits. Product pages help potential customers make informed purchasing decisions.

- **About Us Page**: This page is an opportunity for you to tell your corporate story, introduce key members of your team and showcase your company culture. The About Us page helps build trust and credibility with potential customers.

- **Testimonials and Reviews**: Get your customers to provide feedback, either in written or video form. Testimonials and reviews build trust and credibility and influence purchasing decisions.

- **Resource Center**: Can you give tutorials, how-to guides or other helpful resources? A resource center helps establish your business as an industry leader and will be a valuable source of information for customers.

Some pundits say that to maintain your ranking, you need constantly refreshed and new content. Others point to content they published years ago, which still appears on the first search page. But search isn't everything: many prospects will reach your site after an initial contact, such as at an event or a mailing. And that's where good content will make the sale.

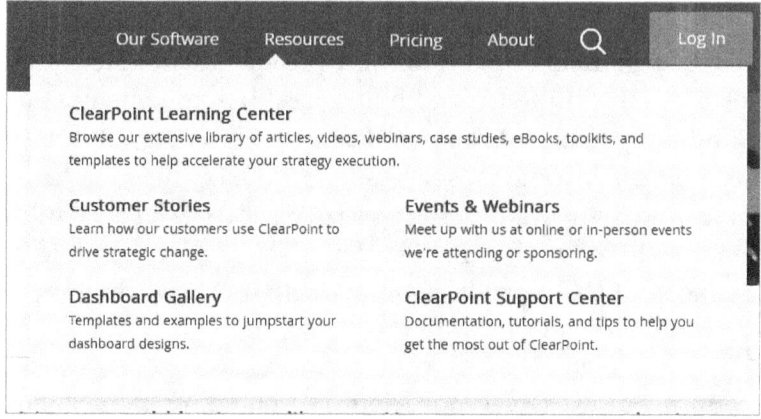

This website provides content that prospects will find useful, including case studies, events and eBooks.

How to augment your own content

1. **Audit your site**. Identify of the above items, if any, are missing.

2. **Commission the content** and put it on your site.

3. **Have a plan** for adding new material regularly.

HOW TO GET MEDIA COVERAGE

Warby Parker, the eyewear company, launched a "Buy a Pair, Give a Pair" program that donated a pair of glasses to someone in need for every pair purchased. The program was picked up by many media outlets and helped to establish the company as a socially responsible business.

As this suggests, getting free media coverage is a good way to raise brand awareness, increase visibility and reach a wider audience without the cost of traditional advertising. Here are some ways you can achieve that:

124

- **Issue a press release:** Do this whenever you have news.

- **Have a unique angle:** Journalists are constantly looking for unique and interesting stories to cover. If your business has an unusual product or work style, it is more likely to get picked up by the media.

- **Build relationships with journalists:** Building relationships with journalists in your industry can be extremely beneficial for getting your business covered in the media. Reach out to journalists and offer valuable insights, and you may find yourself quoted in a news article.

- **Sign up to Help a Reporter Out** (HARO) or a similar site. You can get notified when a journalist asks a question you could answer.

- **Create valuable content:** By creating valuable and shareable content such as blog posts, infographics, and videos, you can get your business noticed by the media and attract them to cover your story.

- **Participate in industry events:** Attending industry events and participating in panels and discussions is an excellent opportunity to network with journalists and get your business in front of them.

- **Use social media:** Social media is a good way to share your content and reach a wider audience. Use social media to share your company's news and updates, and engage with journalists who cover your industry.

- **Do a stunt.** Red Bull hosted a New Moon Party, where people in wingsuits jumped out of helicopters above the tallest building in Los Angeles. The event caused a stir because the jumpers—who were fitted with a sparkler — dropped at sunset, leading people on the ground to think comets or UFOs were descending on the city. A timber merchant that was opening a new branch got a karate expert to break down the (fake) front door to officially open the premises. It got good local publicity.

A Red Bull jumper

WANT TO HEAR A STORY?

Storytelling is a powerful tool that you can use to build stronger relationships with your customers and boost sales. By creating a narrative around your products or services, you can engage customers on an emotional level, creating a deeper connection that leads to increased loyalty and sales.

In particular, you can use it to differentiate your business from your competitors and to create a unique brand identity.

As Seth Godin said, "Marketing is no longer about the stuff that you make, but about the stories you tell."

A carpet cleaning company used a special ingredient, 'saponaria', which had a 'creation myth' around how the founder discovered it. Quite how much the ingredient affected the cleaning process is debatable, but the media loved the story.

Another example is Patagonia, the outdoor clothing business which built its reputation on a commitment to environmental sustainability. The company and tells stories about its efforts to protect the planet through its products and initiatives.

Meanwhile, Coca-Cola has been using storytelling to connect with customers for over a century. From its "Open Happiness" campaign to its holiday campaigns, Coca-Cola has consistently used storytelling to evoke emotions and create a connection with its customers.

How to start your storytelling

1. Trawl the history of your business. Does it have a creation story? Do you have an archive?

2. What distinguishes you from your competitors?

3. Do you or your staff have a distinctive lifestyle?

4. Choose suitable stories to tell. Ensure they're consistent with your brand identity.

5. Get your stories written up and used in your marketing materials.

IDENTIFY CUSTOMER OBJECTIONS

When prospects don't buy from you, it's usually because:

- A competitor is cheaper
- A competitor has a better product
- A competitor has a better brand image
- The prospect is too busy
- The customer can't afford it
- The customer doesn't trust you or know enough about you

- The customer thinks your product won't meet their needs
- The customer thinks the product is too difficult to use or implement
- The customer thinks they don't need it.

By identifying these barriers to purchase, you can take steps to:

- Improve the price/quality/functionality of your product. How can you make your offer more attractive?

- Enhance your communication, including by staff and on the FAQ page of your website.

Identifying and addressing customer objections gives you several benefits:

- **Increased credibility**: By addressing common objections, you can demonstrate a deep understanding of its target audience and their concerns, which will increase customer trust and credibility.

- **Improved conversion rates**: Addressing objections head-on can help to overcome potential roadblocks that may prevent a customer from making a purchase.

- **Better salesmanship**: By anticipating and addressing objections, your sales and support team can be better prepared to handle objections when they arise.

How to meet customer objections

1. **Identify objections** by interviewing customers, by carrying out research, or by asking the sales or customer service team.

2. Put functional **improvements** in place.

3. **Improve your communications** through training and by providing better website information.

THE ETHICS OR VALUES STATEMENT

Are business ethics important? And does it make a difference to proclaim them? The answer is a modified Yes.

Research company Mintel[1] found that 56 percent of US consumers stop buying from companies they believe are unethical. And more than three in five consumers feel that ethical issues are becoming more important (63 percent).

But there is skepticism toward company ethics. Half of Americans agree that marketing products as "ethical" is just a way for companies to manipulate consumers, and that many companies behave ethically in one area while behaving unethically in another.

So, does having a published code help? 95% of both Fortune US 100 and Fortune Global 100 companies have a code of ethics[2], but a review in the *Journal of Business Ethics* found that the code content was predominantly self-defensive, and insufficient in themselves in terms of protecting workers' rights.

What should we conclude from all this? A code of ethics will attract customers. But if it doesn't align with the actuality, it could rebound to your disadvantage.

---

[1]   https://www.mintel.com/press-centre/56-of-americans-stop-buying-from-brands-they-believe-are-unethical/

[2]   https://link.springer.com/article/10.1007/s10551-019-04192-x

Steps to take

1. Identify whether the business would be able to justify a code of ethics.

2. If so, draw up the code, possible including a reference to the company's attitude towards issues such as climate change, labor rights, tax, and the treatment of suppliers and customers.

3. Publicize the statement on your website.

4. Commit to ethical improvements.

5. Be ready to enter into a dialog with critics, and accept responsibility for failings.

REPURPOSE YOUR CONTENT

Too much content sits on office bookshelves or electronic folders, gathering dust. This can happen once a product launch, promotion or exhibition is over. It cost money to produce it originally, so why not make full use of it?

The same applies to content in videos, white papers and articles. It doesn't take much to re-use it in other forms. There are various reasons why you might want to re-purpose your existing content:

*   Maximize the value of your content by getting the most out of each piece you create.

*   Reach new audiences through different channels and formats

*   Reposition your brand and showcase your expertise in different ways.

For example, you could convert a blog post about a new product launch into an infographic to share on social media and highlight the key features of the product in a visually appealing way.

Or you could turn a webinar into a video and upload it to YouTube, to make it accessible to a wider audience. And you could create an eBook by compiling a series of blog posts on a specific topic, making it a comprehensive resource for readers.

To re-purpose content, businesses can start by identifying the most popular or relevant pieces of content and then determine the different ways in which they can be presented to different audiences. Additionally, they can update the content to

In conclusion, re-purposing existing content is an effective way for businesses to maximize the value of your content, reach new audiences and reposition your brand. By using different formats, they can engage with your target audience in new and meaningful ways, and build a strong, consistent brand presence across multiple channels.

How to re-purpose your content

1. Identify all your content, including video and written content.

2. Find out what is the most popular content. Update it if necessary to reflect changes in the industry or add new information to keep it relevant.

3. Identify the various channels your prospects visit (YouTube, Facebook, your website).

4. Work out how you could divide large content into smaller pieces, and expand many small pieces into one larger item.

USE VIDEO

Videos are an effective form to communicate with prospective customers because they let you showcase your products, services, and brand in a dynamic, engaging, and memorable way.

Videos can convey complex information, demonstrate how products work, and evoke emotions that text and still images can't. And these days, it's so much easier to shoot and edit video.

Video can be accessed and watched by anyone, anywhere, and at any time.

Slack, for example, makes maximum use on its website of the moving image. This includes customer testimonial videos, animated graphics that are tantamount to video, and recorded webinars.

You can use videos to drive traffic to your website, where prospective customers can learn more about your products and services. You can share your videos on social media, where they have the potential to reach even more people.

And then there's YouTube. It's a major search engine, with billions of active users. As a result, having a strong video presence on YouTube can help you reach a vast and diverse audience.

How to use video

1. Identify whether additional video will support your marketing goals.

2. If so, understand what kind of video is needed, such as explainers, webinars, testimonials, or product video.

3. Identify on which sites your videos should appear, such as YouTube, Facebook and/or your website.

4. Allocate resources to creating the videos.

Microsoft webinar

HIRE A COPYWRITER

Having persuasive copy on a company's website can greatly enhance the overall user experience and increase conversions. A persuasive copywriter can craft messaging that speaks directly to your target audience and highlights the unique benefits of the company's products or services.

Hiring a professional copywriter can be a wise investment for the business. They will understand the psychology of persuasion and be able to create messaging that resonates.

In comparison with the company's other costs, a copywriter's fees are tiny and short-term; and, unlike most costs, will directly boost your marketing.

Next we move on to promotional tactics

In this chapter, we've been looking at how to communicate with prospects and customers. Now we'll be examining the tactics used to actively persuade people to buy from us.

We'll start with the problem of intangible benefits. These are the ones that customers don't see but are worth emphasizing.

Without promotion, something terrible happens... nothing!
- P. T. Barnum

9. PROMOTION TACTICS

INTANGIBLE BENEFITS

Unlike physical products, you can't touch or feel a service. When you speak to a lawyer or an accountant, or visit an PR agency, it's hard to know what you're going to get.

So, how do you, the service provider, prove to a prospect that they should choose your business?

Intangible benefits are the emotional, psychological benefits, and the perceived value, that a product or service offers its customers. We're talking here about the intangible benefits that can't be seen or touched.

They are often harder to measure and communicate, but are crucial to converting prospects into customers, and building a strong brand identity.

A consultancy practice may focus on the peace of mind, expert advice, and cost savings its services bring. A fitness center may emphasize the sense of community, improved health, and confidence its members gain through their membership.

And it applies to products as well. Most products offer intangible benefits as well as tangible features. If you're selling a can of sardines, one which the customer hasn't seen before, how do you reassure them they'll like it?

Marketing your intangible benefits helps to differentiate your product or service from competitors. A luxury hotel may emphasize its personalized service, exclusive amenities, and elegant décor as part of its branding, while a budget hotel could focus on its affordability and convenience.

Intangible benefits can also be more memorable and impactful for customers. A travel company needs to highlight the life-changing experiences and memories its customers will make on their trips.

As with all marketing activity, your claimed benefits should match the reality. There is no point in mentioning friendly customer service is your receptionists are grumpy and disinterested. Do your practitioners have the look that clients want - a firm handshake, a warm smile, and a cup of coffee? Do they dress appropriately?

Intangible services are people-intensive, which means more scope for variation. That means you need to systematize and audit your intangibles. Standard operating procedures should ensure that follow-up emails get sent, and that all materials have the same look.

Perhaps significant customers should have regular contact, something that is a failing at many professional firms. The audit then checks these procedures are being followed. Technology will help to standardize your operations.

How to define your invisible benefits

1. Define what benefits your service provides.

2. Brainstorm the intangible benefits your clients would like to receive.

3. Understand what reassurance the customer needs before

they commit to you. What refunds or guarantees do you provide?

4. Assess the extent to which the desired intangibles are delivered.

5. Ensure the intangibles are emphasized in your marketing materials. Note how insurance in their imagery insurance companies use metaphors such as umbrellas, while banks may use sturdy rocks.

BUNDLE YOUR PRODUCTS

Bundling lets you sell several additional products together. Let's look at some examples.

SaaS: When you buy Microsoft Office, you get Word, Excel, Outlook and other programs. Some you'll use and others you won't. But it always looks as though you're getting lots for your money.

Cable and streaming services may give you movies, sport, news and cartoons. Or you get a phone and TV bundle.

Restaurants. At many restaurants, a table d'hôte or prix fixe menu will give you a fixed price two- or three-course meal for less than buying each item separately from the a la carte menu. But the restaurateur knows what they're doing. The range is limited, which will encourage you to trade up to the more expensive menu.

The table d'hôte uses off-cut ingredients from the a la carte menu that would otherwise be wasted. It uses fewer ingredients than the a la carte menu, as well as involving simpler recipes and standard portions. So it costs less to produce, and can be bought and prepared in advance. And therefore it reduces the restaurant's costs and increases its margins.

It also brings in customers who are price-sensitive or nervous about choosing from a complicated menu. Bundling works well for restaurants.

Convenience stores provide "Meal Deals" where you get a sandwich, drink and a snack. You pay less for the bundle than you would if you'd bought the three items separately. Sure, you're paying more than if you just bought a sandwich, but most people like a drink to go with their lunch, so it makes sense to go for the bundle because you're getting a great deal, right? And you can choose the most expensive sandwich, you save even more money.

But wait, not so fast. Maybe the retailer knows that most people love a deal. And the idea of getting one over on the retailer is even more appealing.

People think the stupid retailer hasn't worked out how much money the customer is saving. But in reality, the retailer has priced an extra margin into each of these items, to make the bundle look cheap. And so the customer ends up buying three items instead of two.

As can be seen, product bundling offers consumers a package deal where they can buy several items at a discounted price compared to purchasing each product separately. Or so it seems from the outside.

There are several benefits to product bundling. Firstly, it **increases the perceived value of the products** included in the bundle: the customer feels they're getting a better deal compared to buying each item separately.

Secondly, it **encourages customers to purchase complementary products** that they may not have considered before.

It allows you to **offer low-value items that would otherwise be unprofitable,** such as socks, bras or underwear, by selling them in sets.

And finally, bundling can **reduce the cost of production and**

distribution, as you can negotiate better prices with suppliers for buying in bulk and will save on marketing costs by promoting multiple products at once.

How to make a bundle

1. **Identify what products might work together.** Typically, this would be a main product that people must have, plus others that are optional or "nice to have".

2. **Evaluate your average shopping basket**. What would be the effect on sales and profit of bundling? Do your prices need to change?

3. Launch an experiment with one bundle, and review its impact on profit.

MAKE IT SCARCE

Only four left! Sale ends today! When it's gone, it's gone! We've all seen these messages, which are signaling scarcity. Our brain says 'We've got to have it', and common sense goes out the window.

Scarcity is a marketing tool that's been proven to drive sales. It refers to the limited availability of a product, creating a sense of urgency and exclusivity in the minds of consumers.

You can apply the principle of scarcity through limited-time offers. A fast-food chain may offer a special burger that is only available for a limited time. It makes customers want to try it before it's gone. Another example is a retailer offering a limited-time discount on a popular product, creating a sense of urgency for customers to make a purchase before the offer expires.

You can restrict the quantity of a product. You achieve this by promoting a product as a 'limited edition' or by simply limiting the stock available. This creates a sense of exclusivity, as customers feel that they are part of a select group who have access to a unique product.

The principle of scarcity can also improve customer engagement and brand loyalty. By creating a sense of urgency, customers are more likely to share information about a product or service with their friends and family, leading to more word-of-mouth marketing.

Additionally, customers who feel they have access to a unique and exclusive product are more likely to become brand loyalists, as they feel they're part of a special community.

Here are some examples of scarcity:

Limited quantity: Only 10 left.

Introductory Price. Only $20 a month for the first three months. This works for new customers.

Limited time: Only 6 hours left.

Limited bonuses: Buy 2 or more items and get free product.

Limited to existing customers: Make an offer only to people on your list. Give them a coupon.

Limited to a device: Show the offer only on mobile phones, or iPhones.

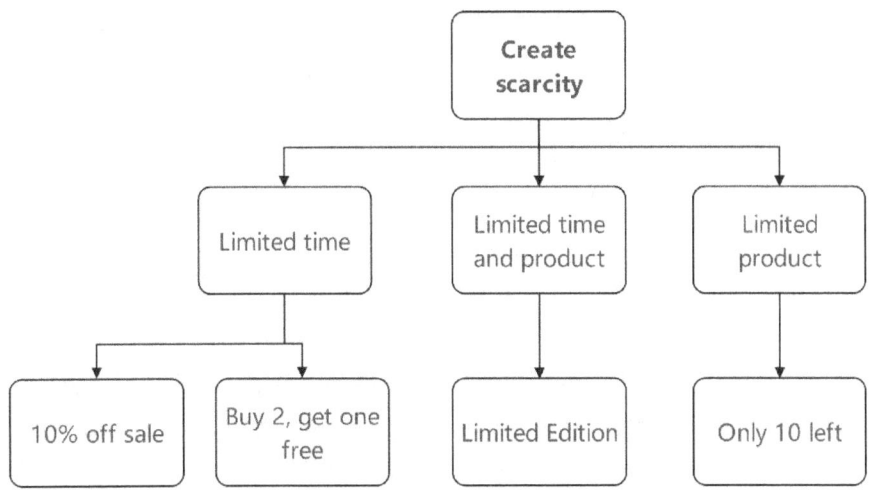

Some of the ways scarcity works

EXCLUSIVITY

Exclusivity is similar to scarcity, but with added cachet. It's Scarcity+.

To achieve this, you need to create a sense of uniqueness around your product. By limiting access to it, you produce a perception of higher value, which results in increased demand, higher prices, and a more loyal customer base.

Some companies achieve this through limited edition products. The Supreme skate wear brand deliberately under-produces its clothes, which creates a big resale market and fosters an exclusive brand identity. When it launches new products, it leads to queues outside its stores, and a sense of urgency and excitement among its customers. In turn, this leads to increased publicity and hype, which can further boost sales.

Luxury brands like Louis Vuitton do the same as Supreme, by limiting the production of their products but also by charging high prices and selling through high-end retailers. This allows them to charge premium prices for their products.

Exclusivity implies that you will exclude "ordinary people", which is why some businesses use membership programs. Sephora offers exclusive perks and discounts to its members.

By charging an annual fee, it creates a sense of exclusivity and prestige around their brand, while also encouraging repeat business from their most loyal customers.

Sephora's first level is free, and offers useful but limited benefits. To get into the top tier, you have to spend $1,000 a year, but that gives you first access to products, as well as invitations to exclusive events.

Queues outside Supreme. Image: Pavel Kaczorowski

GIVE AWAY FREE STUFF

Giving away a product or service for free to your target audience will serve to generate awareness and sales. They can create a buzz and increase brand visibility, because people are more likely to talk about a brand that has given them something for free.

A food and beverage company might give away a free sample of its new product at a local grocery store. Customers who try the product are more likely to remember the brand and purchase it again in the future.

Low-cost freebies such as pens or shopping bags are a common sight at trade shows. Promotional pens may remain on a buyer's desk for many months, reminding the person who to contact when the need arises.

Another example is a clothing company offering a discount coupon with every purchase, encouraging customers to return and make another purchase. This can create brand loyalty and repeat business.

A skincare company might offer a free sample of a new product to entice customers to try it out. This not only gives the customer a chance to experience the product for themselves, but it also positions the company as a generous and trustworthy brand.

In the tech industry, companies often offer a free 30-day trial for their products to encourage users to try them out and eventually make a purchase. Users are more likely to buy a product they have already had a chance to use and become familiar with.

Overall, giveaways and freebies are a low-cost way for businesses to create positive associations with your brand, drive sales, and acquire new customers. When executed well, they can be a valuable component of your overall marketing strategy.

GIVE TO GET

People are more likely to purchase from a company if they feel that they have received something of value from them first. That's the principle of "give to get" or "reciprocity".

This is one step up from handing out simple freebies, and is typically more targeted.

You can apply reciprocity this by providing a product sample, valuable content or information, or by showing support and understanding.

Give to get is especially relevant to marketing communications. People don't want to be sold to. They want advice and information. These days, selling looks sleezy in the eyes of some people.

Reciprocity builds trust and rapport with potential customers. By giving something of value, you demonstrate that you care about them and are willing to invest in building a relationship with them. This can lead to increased brand loyalty and higher conversion rates.

It can also help you stand out in a crowded market. By offering something unique and valuable, you can differentiate themselves from your competitors and capture the attention of potential customers. For anyone visiting various car dealers looking for a vehicle, the helpfulness or otherwise of the staff will affect their decision.

You might provide a free online course to help educate your potential customers. This demonstrates your expertise and commitment to helping your customers succeed, which will increase the likelihood of the customer choosing to do business with you in the future.

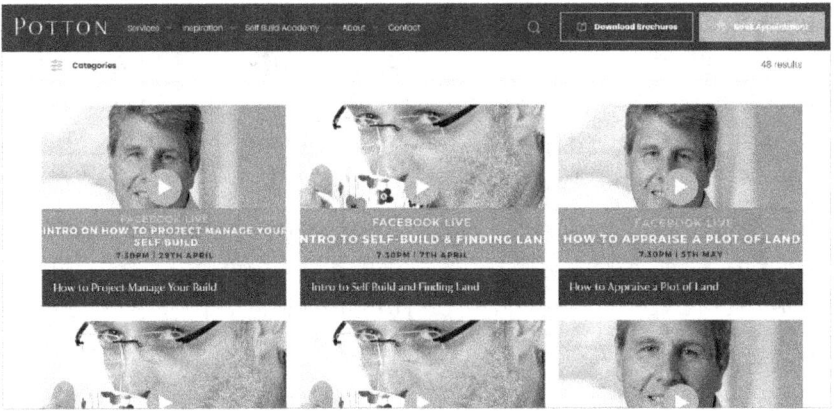

Prerecorded webinars by a construction company provide free advice to self-builders - an example of 'Give to Get'.

FREE CONSULTATION

Giving free advice is a version of the "Give to Get" tactic we discussed earlier. You can use it to win clients, especially if you're in a service business.

Providing a 30-minute consultation allows you to showcase your expertise and demonstrate your ability to add value to the client's business. This helps to build trust and establish a relationship with potential clients, which is essential in winning their business.

A financial consultant can offer a free consultation to small business owners to help them identify areas where they could improve their finances. During this consultation, the consultant can provide valuable insights and recommendations that the business owner might not have considered.

This could lead to the business owner hiring the consultant to help implement the recommended changes, which would result in cost savings and improved financial performance.

A digital marketing agency can offer a free website audit to potential clients. This would provide a comprehensive analysis of the client's website, including recommendations for improving the site's user experience, search engine optimization, and overall performance. Much of this can be done using software.

By offering this service for free, the agency can demonstrate its expertise and build trust with the potential client, which could lead to a long-term relationship and the acquisition of new clients.

By offering a free consultation or service, you differentiate your business from your competitors and establish yourself as a valuable resource in your industry.

How to implement a free consultation program

1. **Identify the problems** and uncertainties your prospects have.

2. Decide what advice you will give and how to structure it.

3. Set up a 'free consultation' page on your website.

4. **Include a self-booking form.** On it, ask questions that give you information about the prospect, including their needs and aspirations.

5. Ensure you are staffed up to deal with inquiries.

6. To ensure prospects become clients, diagnose their problems and explain the impact they have on their business. But **don't explain the "how".**

7. **Limit the meeting to the 30 minutes** or whatever time you've offered. Your time is valuable. And cutting it short leaves them wanting more.

8. To stay in touch with inquirers, **have a follow up system**, such as an email sequence.

USE FOMO AND LOSS AVERSION

"Fear of Missing Out" (FOMO) and "Loss Aversion" are two psychological principles that are widely used in marketing.

FOMO refers to the feeling of anxiety or regret that people experience when they think they might miss out on an opportunity, such as a new product launch, a limited-time offer or a once-in-a-lifetime experience.

Loss Aversion is more or less the same thing. It refers to people's tendency to prefer avoiding losses over getting equivalent gains.

In marketing, we use this principle to show a customer that they'll lose out on something valuable if they don't take advantage of a particular offer.

You can do this by creating a sense of urgency around your products or services, using phrases such as "limited-time offer" or "only a few left in stock." You can motivate customers to make a purchase, often without them even realizing why they made the decision.

A clothing brand might announce a flash sale with a limited number of items available at a discounted price. This motivates customers to make a purchase before the items sell out.

Booking.com often shows how many rooms are left on a specific day. And the customer's fear of losing the booking encourages them to take action.

How to use FOMO and loss aversion

1. **Display offers that are time-limited**. This will motivate customers to purchase within that time window to avoid losing out.

147

2. **Let people know you have a limited number of products or service packages available**. Customers will be motivated to buy now, so they don't lose out. You can see this effect every year on Black Friday.

3. **Add a count-down timer or stock count** to your website. The visual reminders will encourage customers to buy before it's too late.

4. **But don't overuse this** and other Sale tactics. Offering them too often encourages people to purchase only during sales. And excessive Sale banners may cheapen your offer or make customers feel they are being manipulated.

OPTIMIZE YOUR PRODUCT LAUNCH

Some organisations simply pump out new products, do a small bit of launch marketing, and go on to the next project. That doesn't give the product the best send-off. We need to commit time and money to the product launch; and that can mean launching fewer products and spending more time on each.

Product launches are critical moments in an organization's life: they can determine the success or failure of a product. Hence, optimizing product launches is crucial to gaining more awareness and revenue. Here are some ways you can do that:

- **Conduct Market Research**: Understand the target audience and your preferences, what the competitors are offering, and the potential of the product in the market. This information can help you create a product that meets the needs of the target market and set realistic goals for the launch.

- **Build a set of marketing activities**: A well-thought-out marketing strategy that includes a mix of digital and traditional advertising, influencer partnerships and public relations can help create buzz around the product and drive sales.

- **Create Excitement**: Offer pre-launch promotions, exclusive access to the product, and launch events to create excitement and anticipation among customers.

- **Foster Customer Engagement**: Encourage customers to share their experiences with the product on social media and other platforms. This can help increase brand awareness and reach new audiences.

The Harry Potter franchise was built upon a strong marketing strategy that involved creating a sense of mystery and excitement through a series of events and promotions leading up to the launch of the books and films. This helped generate massive awareness and revenue for the franchise.

10,000 girls aged eight to 12 lined up to audition for the character of Modesty in the movie "Fantastic Beasts and Where to Find Them".

How to achieve a better launch

1. **Identify what new products** and services are in your pipeline.

2. **Create a plan** that will build excitement and awareness.

3. **Assign team members** to execute the launch.

Seek Social Proof

These days people are less impressed with advertising, or what Seth Godin called "interruption marketing". They're more cynical about advertisers' claims, and much more inclined to believe friends and other users.

And so we're in a world where social proof creates sales. According to a Northwestern University study, the likelihood for someone to buy a product with five reviews is 270% greater than for a product with no reviews. But after five reviews, the effect tails off. And the propensity to buy is much greater for higher price purchases.

Reviews need to be on independent sites, according to the Baymard Institute. Customers will discount reviews written by your customers on your own websites. But user generated content, for example videos showing how customers use your product are influential. So are celebrity endorsements, case studies and social media influencers.

And consumers expect to see some negative reviews. They smell a rat if they're missing.

Before Amazon, companies shied away from showing negative reviews. People said they hurt sales. Then in 2004 Jeff Bezos, Amazon's CEO, decided the company would collect as many product reviews as it could. Bezos reckoned that reviews would help boost trust and would lead to a higher conversion. Bezos said:

"When we pioneered customer reviews, it was incredibly controversial. I got letters from publishers saying, 'You don't understand your business. You make money when you sell things. Take down those negative customer reviews.'

Amazon recognizes the importance of its reviews, and it's one of the reasons people flock to the site. It isn't accidental that reviews appear in a prominent position for every product.

Similarly, Airbnb displays guest reviews and ratings to help guests choose the best listings. These reviews and ratings act as social proof and help build trust and credibility with potential customers.

How to get social proof

1. **Systematize the process** of asking customers to give a review, especially on third party sites. If you aren't currently asking for reviews, it takes courage. Businesses fear the risk of negative reviews. But good products and service will produce positive reviews. And many third-party sites let you challenge unfair reviews.

2. **Find a celebrity** who resonates with your customers. See if they're open to endorsing your products.

3. Seek out some social media influencers who write about your market.

4. **Claim your company profile** on Google Business Profile, Facebook. Also claim any relevant sites such as Yelp, TripAdvisor, Better Business Bureau and Trustpilot.

5. **Get case studies written**, if that is relevant to your market.

6. **Assign team members** to be responsible for seeking reviews and managing them.

RUN COMPETITIONS

Running competitions can increase awareness and sales for you by creating a buzz around the brand and attracting new customers. You can use competitions to build brand recognition and encourage people to engage with your business in a fun and interactive way.

When you run a competition, it can generate attention, both online and offline, as people share the competition details with their friends and family. This can help to increase the reach of the business and bring in new customers who may not have heard of the business before.

A real-life example of this is the "Share a Coke" campaign run by Coca-Cola. The campaign encouraged people to buy Coca-Cola products with their friends' names on the packaging and share photos of the drinks on social media. The competition helped to increase brand awareness and sales as people were incentivized to engage with the brand and share it with their friends.

Another example is the "12 Days of Christmas" competition run by many businesses. These competitions offer a different prize each day for 12 days, often in conjunction with promotional offers and partner businesses. People are encouraged to keep coming back to see what the next prize would be.

How to run a successful competition

1. **Have a clear goal**. The competition must have a purpose. Do you want to create excitement and brand awareness, position the brand, or simply collect email addresses?

2. **Obey social media rules**. For example, your Facebook page can be closed if you ask people to share the competition on their page. Read what the platforms say about running competitions.

3. **Obey state licensing and permit laws**. Many forbid you from requiring a purchase.

4. **Offer a great prize**. Make it something that your audience really wants. Have enough smaller prizes to give many people a chance to win.

5. **Make it easy to enter**. The simplest method is just to collect an email address. Asking people to write a poem will limit the number of entries.

6. **Promote the competition widely**. And follow up with publicity in local media about the winners, with their approval.

7. Include terms and conditions that **limit your liability**.

LET CUSTOMERS CREATE YOUR CONTENT

Calvin Klein invites customers to post photos on social media of themselves in Calvin Klein products, using the #MyCalvins hashtag.

The company then uses some of these images on its website, with a link to the product page. Customers can then buy the look for themselves. This does several things. It makes the fashion brand seem real and approachable.

It provides social proof. It garners extra content, all of which is authentic - something that users prize. It shows appreciation for its customers. It builds a tribe. It creates sales opportunities. And it costs the business nothing.

User-generated content (UGC) taps into the social media zeitgeist. It encourages users to produce and share their own content, whether reviews, photos, videos, and social media posts.

You can also get UGC through customer feedback and surveys. This can help you better understand your customers' needs and preferences.

How to get user generated content

1. **Ask users to create images or videos of them using your product**, and share them on social media. Use a unique hashtag, so you can find it.

2. Identify the skills or experiences your customers gain through using your products or services.

3. **Set up a community site** where visitors can ask questions and get them answered by others. If necessary, send request for answers to your email list.

User-generated content for Calvin Klein.

4. Ensure you acquire the intellectual rights to the use of the material.

5. Set a team member to review and use the content you receive.

COMPARATIVE ADVERTISING

Burger King has long been known for running ads that compare its burgers with those of its rival MacDonald's, as the poster below shows.

This is comparative advertising, typically used by No. 2 brands that have a competitive advantage over the brand leader, and are determined to promote it.

Burger King compares its burger with McDonald's

Comparative advertising compares a company's products or services with those of its competitors, with the aim of demonstrating superiority and encouraging customers to choose your products.

There are many ways to run comparative ads. For example, you might simply have a table showing the functions in a side-by-side comparison with your competitor.

And consider the impact on consumers. They prefer to see lighthearted campaigns, so it may be wise to soften the edge of your campaign with humor.

Advantages of comparative advertising include:

- **Increased awareness and recall**: By directly comparing products, customers are more likely to remember your brand and its features.

- **Demonstrated superiority**: By highlighting the differences between your products and competitors', you can demonstrate why your products are superior and more valuable.

- **Encouragement of brand switching**: If your 's product is seen to be superior to the competition, it will encourage customers to switch from the competitor's brand to your own.

However, comparative advertising also comes with some risks, including:

- **Legal issues**: If the claims you make are not accurate or truthful, you may face legal action from the competitor.

- **Damaged relationships with competitors**: Comparative advertising may damage relationships with your competitors, which could harm future business opportunities.

- **Decreased credibility**: If the claims made in comparative advertising are perceived as false or misleading, it may damage your credibility and reputation.

- **Promote a competitor's product**. By showing your competitor's product in your ads, you are boosting their awareness. Always choose a brand that is better known than your own.

How to implement comparative advertising

1. Assess whether you have a competitive advantage over your competitor.

2. Review the advantages and risks of running a comparative ad campaign.

3. Brief your ad agency and assess the creative executions.

4. Get legal advice.

5. Decide whether to run the campaign. If you do, monitor the impact.

HIRE A CELEBRITY OR INFLUENCER

If you have $40 million to spare, you could hire George Clooney to star in your commercials, as Nestle has over the years. And if you're well known, as George Clooney is, you might decide that dressing up in silly clothes is worth the money they pay you.

That's the Faustian deal between companies and celebrities. Nestle has done well from the endorsements, albeit rocked by news that in Guatemala child laborers were picking and hauling heavy beans for Nespresso as they worked six days a week.

George Clooney advertising Nespresso

Using influencers, media personalities, or celebrity endorsements to promote a product brings several advantages. They often have a large and engaged following on social media platforms, which can lead to increased visibility and awareness of the product.

They also create credibility and trust in your product, as their endorsement is perceived as a sign of quality. This is known as "transference," whereby the positive attributes of the influencer, media personality, or celebrity are transferred to the product.

Another advantage of using influencer marketing is the ability to reach a specific target audience. Influencers often have a niche following, allowing brands to target specific demographics, such as beauty, fitness, or lifestyle.

How to use celebrity endorsement

1. Decide whether a celebrity or influencer could lend credibility and excitement to your brand.

2. Determine your budget. Celebrities aren't cheap.

3. Short list suitable individuals. You will probably need to use a celebrity management agency. Ideally the celebrity should have some link with your product, such as athletes and a sports brand.

4. Agree the scope of the engagement. A single speech will be a lot cheaper, but less enduring than a long-lasting TV campaign.

5. Sign the contract and launch the campaign.

REDUCE THE RISK

When you walk down the aisles of a supermarket, you can see people hesitating in front of the shelves. It's partly because they have a choice, but partly because they're worried whether the product is right for them.

What if they don't like the taste? What if they can't cook it right? Which size if right for their family? It's called the FUD factor (Fear, Uncertainty and Doubt).

And that is for a very simple product. As the price tag gets bigger, so the risk of making a bad decision grows. If you don't like the car or sofa you've bought, you can't just take it back to the dealer, and ask for your money back.

Every time someone decides to buy your product, there's a lingering doubt at the back of their mind. You need to address the consumer's concerns, or it will linger and fester, and hinder the sale.

One thing you should do, therefore, is to reduce the risk for the customer. There are many ways to do this.

Offer a guarantee or warranty. While most companies do this, it's often done to comply with legal requirements, and sounds defensive. If you offer longer or less conditional guarantees, it helps to reduce the client's anxiety. Surprisingly, a longer guarantee doesn't seem to increase refunds. Quite the reverse: customers don't feel pressurized to return the product in the first 30 days, so the thought of asking for a refund gets pushed to the back of their mind.

Demonstrate adequate after sales support. If the customer knows they can contact you for help, they will be reassured.

Provide a trial. You can supply samples of the product, or give people a trial period to use it.

Customer reviews and testimonials. See "Seek social proof".

Use clear product descriptions and specifications. By providing as much information as possible about your product, you can help customers make informed decisions and reduce the risk of dissatisfaction. Ensure your packaging contains everything the customer needs to know. Make the fonts large enough to read. Show step by step images, if appropriate. Don't make assumptions about the user's knowledge. Assume they are a "newbie".

Reducing the risk in projects

In tailor-made projects such as construction, the cost and risk are high, and the finished product will only be visible at the end of the job. Here are ways to reduce the risk:

Explain the process. Hence you should show in detail how the process will work, what the milestones are, and what the deliverables are.

Evidence the finished job. Show artists' impressions of the finished product.

Chunk the cost. You can also set stage payments, which means the client will not risk all the money at once.

Engage stakeholders. In a complex sale, many people are involved in the final decision. They may have quite unexpected issues, such as departmental friction or hidden agendas. Ensure you speak to them, understand their concerns and seek to allay them. Give the client's project manager the evidence they need to convince their doubtful colleagues.

Use proxy evidence of expertise. This can be staff experience or qualifications, previous work or references.

Provide quantitative data. Show you have considered the job in detail, with research reports, studies and assessments.

FOLLOW UP

You've made contact with a prospective supplier, explained what you need, and been promised a proposal or quotation.

And that's the last you hear from them.

It's not that they don't want your business, rather that they don't have a system for ensuring that quotations aren't dispatched. It happens more often than people imagine. The sales team send requests to head office, and it languishes in someone's inbox.

And if you don't get the promised information, you'll assume they're either disorganized or don't care enough about their work. You're unlikely to chase them for the information.

The same applies to contacts made at an exhibition or networking event. Promises are made but not kept.

But let's say they manage to send you the details you need. Hurray. But time goes by, other more pressing problems arise, and you don't quite get around to making a decision.

Weeks pass, and they don't follow up. So you start talking to other suppliers, some of whom seem more organized.

This scenario shows that good follow-up is essential. And it's not just for big projects. With today's marketing automation and CRM (customer relationship management) software, it is easy to set in train a follow-up process that impresses prospects and customers. And inquiries should be repeatedly followed up until the prospect explicitly states that they are not going to use you.

When customers feel that their concerns are being heard and addressed, they are more likely to feel valued and satisfied with their overall experience. Follow-up can be done in a variety of ways, including by phone, email, or in-person. Here are some examples:

By phone: After a customer has made a purchase, your representative can call them to ensure they received their product and are satisfied with it. If the customer has any issues or concerns, the representative can work to resolve them over the phone. This shows the customer that you're committed to their satisfaction and are willing to take the extra step to ensure they are happy.

By email: If a customer has reached out with a question or concern, you can send a follow-up email to let them know that you've received their inquiry and it is being addressed. The email should also provide a timeline for when the customer can expect a resolution. This helps the customer feel that their issue is being taken seriously and that you're working to find a solution. Use autoresponder emails to keep in touch with the prospect or client.

How to implement a follow-up system

1. Assess how prospects make contact, including by phone, email and face to face.

2. Define how those contacts are logged, and how follow ups are made.

3. Where the system depends on humans, see how that process can be automated.

4. Implement new fool-proof systems where appropriate.

INCENTIVIZE PEOPLE TO PROMOTE YOUR PRODUCTS

Why market your products when you could get others to do it for you? That's the promise of an affiliate or referral program.

In the online world, there are plenty of websites where the site owner will review your product and give visitors a link to your site. If the visitor subsequently buys your product, the originating site gets a share of the revenue.

Setting up an affiliate program has several benefits for your business. It increases brand exposure as affiliates promote your products or services to their audience. It drives more traffic to your 's website, potentially leading to more sales.

Thirdly, it can be a cost-effective way to acquire new customers as you only pay your affiliate when a sale is made. Finally, it builds trust and credibility as affiliates are more likely to promote products they have used and trust themselves.

Amazon's affiliate program allows people to earn a commission by promoting Amazon products on their own websites. The Commission Junction platform connects businesses with affiliates, helping to streamline the affiliate program process. And Rakuten Marketing offers a range of affiliate marketing solutions, including a tracking and reporting system.

How to set up an affiliate program

1. Decide whether it supports your marketing strategy.

2. Review affiliate program apps and their costs. Select one.

3. Identify products your affiliates might want to promote.

4. Decide how much revenue you will cede to your affiliates.

5. Assign someone to manage affiliates and promote the program,

SPONSOR TO GET NOTICED

Sponsoring a community, sporting, or arts organization or

team can bring you a range of benefits.

It builds brand awareness and loyalty among the target audience, because associate your business with the positive experiences they have with the sponsored organization. If you sponsor a local sports team and provide equipment for their games, the community is likely to remember your generosity and buy from you in return.

Sponsorship gives you an opportunity to build relationships with influencers. You can network with other local businesses, politicians and community leaders, helping to build your reputation and increase your visibility.

You can also use the sponsorship as a platform to launch new products or services and receive valuable feedback from your target audience.

But there are also pitfalls to consider when sponsoring an organization. If it is involved in controversy, it can have a negatively effect on your reputation. Nike has a long list of athletes who were subsequently disgraced, including Tiger woods (sex scandal), Oscar Pistorius (murder), and Lance Armstrong (doping scandal); while Adidas cut its links with Kanye West, now known as Ye, (white supremacist and anti-semitism).

It also works the other way. Museums and galleries that have taken sponsorship from oil companies or gambling businesses have faced criticism. And those who took money from Purdue Pharma, makers of Oxycontin, suffered major attacks on their reputation.

Additionally, there is a risk that the sponsorship will not deliver the expected results or return on investment. This can happen if the target audience is not engaged or if the sponsorship is not effectively marketed.

Sponsorship is one of those marketing activities that seems to benefit either very large or hyper local businesses, with much less in between This may be because the results are hard to evaluate, and comes after traditional advertising and sales promotion have been exhausted.

How to set up a sponsorship deal

1. Identify what interests your customers or clients

2. Review what benefits might accrue from sponsorship, and how it might fit into your marketing strategy.

3. Identify how much money you can spend on sponsorship and what return on investment you would expect, where possible.

4. Shortlist and select a suitable beneficiary.

5. Agree what exposure you require.

6. Get a contract signed.

7. Implement the sponsorship.

CREATE EVENTS

Our digital marketing world seems so neat and tidy. With its metrics and reports, it feels so straightforward and controlled. But it's an artificial and two-dimensional space that lacks the personal contact than many humans value. What about the real world that customers inhabit?

One way to get close to existing customers and find new ones is through events. You can either attend local networking events, which even large businesses do, or set up your own.

Events allow you to build relationships and partnerships that can lead to increased sales, referrals and new business opportunities. Dreamforce, the annual Salesforce conference attracts thousands of attendees each year, providing an opportunity for businesses to connect with potential customers, learn about developments in their industry and network with other companies.

Physical events also offer the chance to showcase products and services in a way that is not possible through other marketing channels. The World Mobile Congress (WMC) in Barcelona is a gathering of global mobile phone manufacturers that allows them to showcase their latest devices, software and services. It provides a platform for businesses to demonstrate their products to a global audience and gain valuable exposure in the marketplace.

Creating social events such as award ceremonies, lunches, and festivals also offer businesses the opportunity to build their brand, connect with customers and create positive associations. Legal and General, an insurance business, runs roadshows around the UK, offering talks, technology updates, and the ability for brokers to talk to lenders, plus food and refreshments. The company also runs an awards ceremony.

However, events take a lot of organising and resources. And to be effective you need be in it for the long haul.

How to create a worthwhile event or attend others'

1. Review what events take place in your industry, and what ones your customers currently attend.

2. Identify what benefits or information your customers might value that they aren't getting.

3. From 1 and 2, decide what kind of event you might be able to run.

4. Define the costs and possible benefits, and decide whether

you should create your own event or piggy back on others' events.

EXHIBITIONS AND TRADE SHOWS

If you're looking for ways to boost your company's visibility and increase your customer base, participating in a trade show or exhibition is something to consider. Here's why:

They provide a platform for you to showcase your products or services to a large audience. This is an opportunity for you to make a lasting impression on potential customers and build brand awareness. In addition, these fairs and shows allow you to connect with other businesses in your industry, which can lead to valuable partnerships and collaborations.

It also gives you the chance to get closer to your target market. You can learn more about your customers' needs and preferences by engaging with them directly, which can help you refine your marketing strategies and improve your products.

Finally, exhibitions and shows are a great way to generate leads and drive sales. By offering special promotions or discounts to attendees, you can encourage people to try your products or services and convert them into loyal customers. Plus, the connections you make at these events can lead to long-term business relationships and repeat business.

How to gain more business by exhibiting at a show

1. Identify suitable exhibitions.

2. Understand your objective, and design your presence around that.

3. Train your staff on good exhibition techniques, such as what to say, how to collect contacts' details, why they

should not have food and drinks on the stand, and how to avoid blocking visitor access.

4. Provide experiences on the stand, such as video and demonstrations.

5. Inform people on your mailing list in advance.

6. Provide give-aways with your logo or contact details.

Next we investigate how to run profitable Sales

The Sale has always been with us, whether to clear out old stock or an attempt to bring more people into our store. But all too often the Sale is a desperate attempt to generate revenue. We need to make it work to our advantage, so that's what we cover in next chapter.

All business success rests on something labeled a sale, which at least momentarily weds company and customer.
- Tom Peters

10. SALE TACTICS

HOW TO RUN A SALE

The main purpose of a Sale is to stimulate demand by offering your products or services at a reduced price for a limited period of time. Advantages of using a sale include the following:

- **Boost immediate sales**: By offering a discount, you can attract customers who might not have otherwise made a purchase.

- **Clear out inventory**: A Sale will let you get rid of old or excess inventory, which frees up space for new products and brings in useful revenue.

- **Attract new customers**: Sales can be a way to attract new customers and introduce them to your products or services.

- **Increase revenue during low quiet periods**: Most businesses have seasonal peaks and troughs. Running a sale in a low period can keep machines running, prevent staff layoffs, and increase revenue.

However, sales also have some drawbacks:

- **Condition customers to wait for sales**: If you run sales too frequently, customers may start to wait for them before making a purchase, leading to decreased sales during non-sale periods.

- **Damage to your brand image**: If you constantly offer discounts and sales, it can damage the perceived value of your products and undermine their brand image. The whole point of Gucci, Prada or Louis Vuitton is that they're expensive and therefore inaccessible to the majority of people.

- **Decrease your profit margins**: While sales can increase sales, they also decrease the profit margins on each item sold.

How to run a profitable Sale

1. Understand why you want to run a Sale, and what you want the outcomes to be.

2. Identify the right time to run a Sale. For example, you might want to run it just after people have been paid.

3. Consider what product should be put on Sale. You shouldn't give customers money off products they would have bought anyway. That's just throwing money away.

4. Launch the Sale.

5. Review the effect of the Sale. What was the impact on profit? There is no point in simply running faster just to stand still.

FLASH SALE

With a Flash Sale you discount your products at a heavily reduced price, typically for a short period of time, usually 24 to 72 hours.

Flash sales increase sales by creating a sense of urgency and scarcity among shoppers. This drives customers to make a purchase quickly before the sale ends, as they don't want to miss out on a good deal.

Additionally, flash sales can help generate buzz and excitement around a product or brand, as people are more likely to share the sale with their friends and family.

An example of a successful flash sale is the annual Prime Day event by Amazon. During Prime Day, Amazon offers deep discounts on a wide range of products for its Prime members, including electronics, home goods, and fashion.

Another example is the flash sales offered by Groupon, where users can find limited-time deals on local businesses, including restaurants, spas, and activities. These events have been successful in driving sales and attracting new customers to these businesses.

BOGOF AND ITS ALTERNATIVES

Standing for "Buy One Get One Free", BOGOF (also known as BOGO) is a promotional device in which you offer customers a free product with every product they purchase. Its advantages include the following:

- **Increased sales**: By offering a free product, you can encourage customers to buy more, resulting in an increase in overall sales.

- **Attracting new customers**: BOGOF offers can be an effective way to lure new customers and get them to try your products.

- **Clearing out inventory**: You can use these offers to clear out excess inventory, reducing the risk of waste and maximizing profits.

Fast food restaurants typically offer "Buy One, Get One Free" deals on burgers or "buy one large pizza, get one small pizza free." Supermarkets also often have BOGOF promotions on products such as groceries, cleaning supplies, and personal care items.

There are many variations on BOGOF. They include:

Buy two, get the third free (BTGTF). This reduces the bargain from an extra 100% to 50%, and thus reduces your cost, but it remains attractive. It is also known as "Buy three for the price of two".

Buy three for only $5. For example, customers pay $2 for one pen, whereas they can get three pens for only $5. This greatly increases the value of the purchase to you.

Buy one, get one half price. This reduces the cost to you, but is still a good deal for the consumer.

Buy this and get a free that. For example, buy a phone and get a free case.

Buy this and get a sample free. This works well in toiletries and cosmetics. It introduces the customer to a product they haven't used before, and could lead to future revenue.

Buy this and get X% off that. This works for complementary items. For example, the customer buys a sofa and gets 30% of a matching armchair.

Which products are suitable?

Consumables: If customers use the product regularly, such as shampoo, they'll buy more to stock up. But this means they will take twice as long before they buy again.

Products that complement each other. You can offer the deal across a range of fruit or snacks.

Items with at least a 50% margin. A margin is your profit after accounting for costs. If your product's margin is 50%, and one of your items is free, your sale is break-even. So you neither make or lose money on the deal. Try to include at least one product with a higher margin higher than 50% to make a profit.

Impact on profit

A BOGOF or BTGTF promotion can have a positive or negative impact on your profitability, depending on how you set it up.

If the promotion attracts more customers to the store or boosts your sales, it may increase your revenue, offsetting the cost of the free product.

However, if it means customers purchase fewer products overall, or if the costs of the giveaway are higher than the increase in revenue, it will decrease profitability.

Ultimately, the impact on profitability will depend on various factors, such as the cost of your products, your target customers, the margin on each product, and the marketing and operational costs associated with the promotion.

Such promotions require the customer to buy more than they would normally do. Doubling the revenue may outweigh the cost of giving away the third product.

Bear in mind that what you pay for the product is less than what you charge the consumer. In a restaurant, for example, the cost of food is only 25% - 40% of your total costs.

How to run a profitable price promotion

1. Run BOGOF promotions only for a limited time period, to

create urgency. It stops customers getting used to discounted prices.

2. Test your BOGOGF promotion. Sales must increase to the point where profit is no lower than before the promotion, and ideally should be higher.

3. Time your promotions strategically, such as during the holiday season or during events like Black Friday.

4. Clearly display any conditions or limitations of the sale.

5. Choose your products carefully. They should complement each other and suit your target audience.

THE CROSS-SELL

In a cross-sell, you promote a related product or service to a customer who is already interested in buying a product.

- A customer is buying a mattress: offer them bedlinen or pillows.

- They're buying a yoga mat. Suggest a book on yoga.

- They're getting a new phone. Offer them insurance, a case or ear buds.

- They're buying a power drill. Suggest drill bits.

- And there's the traditional offer in a fast-food outlet: "Do you want fries with that?"

The essence of the cross sell is that it's a complementary product or useful service. If they're buying a bike, they might want a bike rack for a car, but they wouldn't want car wash items.

Online stores can offer a cross-sell a section called "Customers also bought". Or "frequently bought together". At shoe stores, customers are usually offered shoe polish.

Adding a cross-sell in a shopping cart benefits you in several ways:

- **Increased sales revenue**: By offering related products, cross-selling can increase the total order value, thereby boosting the business's sales revenue.

- **Improved customer satisfaction**: By suggesting complementary products, you help customers find the right products they need and make the purchasing process more convenient and efficient.

- **Better inventory management**: Cross-selling helps you move inventory faster, and reduce the risk of stock obsolescence.

How to implement a cross sell

1. Map your product categories. Identify your main products and their related add-ons.

2. Ensure that the add-ons, accessories or supplementary products are shown with each main product.

3. If in a bricks and mortar store, ensure that staff understand what add-ons they could offer. A shoe shop customer is usually offered shoe polish.

THE UPSELL

If you want to increase your average order value, the upsell is a good solution. Electrical equipment, from vacuum cleaners to lawn mowers, comes in a range of options. And at some time we've all bought a piece of equipment that was under-powered or insufficiently flexible.

The same applies to almost all items, from a cheap tin of beans upwards. Hence the value of an upsell. At times we save the customer from themselves.

In an online transaction, you can compare product features in a table, emphasizing the advantages of the better product. And in a bricks-and-mortar store, the shop assistant can explain why the more expensive version might be a better buy.

Offering finance or installments is a good way to reduce the customer's pain in the upsell. And telling the customer, "It's only $25 more a month to get the Sport model" makes it easier for the customer than saying "The Sports model will cost you $2,000 extra."

Here are some of the benefits of having an upsell strategy:

Upsells give you an opportunity to increase the value of each transaction. By offering customers additional products or services, you increase the amount of money they earn from each sale. This can be particularly beneficial if your business has low margins or you struggle to attract repeat customers.

They can be a cost-effective way to increase revenue. Rather than spending money on acquiring new customers, you can focus on maximizing the value of each transaction by offering upsells. This approach can result in a higher return on investment and a more profitable business.

They can help build customer loyalty. By offering customers products that are more relevant to their needs, you establish a stronger relationship with them.

How to create an upsell

1. Identify which of your products have a range of options.

2. Ensure that sales assistants or support staff explain the benefits of products in the same category that offer more functionality or better performance.

3. Ensure that your website has the functionality to provide upsells.

4. Make the upsell relatively inexpensive compared with the main product, such as 10% or 15% more. A bigger increase in the cost of the upsell could irritate the customer.

Next we look at online tactics

Content management systems (CMS) like WordPress have given us an extraordinary range of toys to play with, from popups to ready-made chat programs, mostly at bargain-basement prices.

We'll be investigating some of the main tools, but first let's deal with some basics of digital marketing.

As the world becomes a more digital place,
we cannot forget about the human connection.
- Adam Neumann

11. DIGITAL TACTICS

DON'T RELY ON FACEBOOK

It may sound a statement of the obvious, but every business needs a website.

Yet just over a quarter of small businesses (28%) have no website. They either have no digital presence, or regard their Facebook page as adequate.

You shouldn't rely solely on platforms like Facebook, Amazon or eBay for several reasons:

- **Dependence**: Relying on these platforms makes you dependent and vulnerable: these platforms can change their policies, fees, or even terminate your account without notice.

- **Branding**: When selling on social media sites, your brand image is diluted and may not be accurately represented, limiting your ability to differentiate you from competitors or build brand loyalty.

- **Data ownership**: By replying on platforms, you don't own the customer data and have limited control over how it is used. That makes it harder to build a direct relationship with your customers and retain them.

- **Limited control**: Platforms like Amazon, eBay, etc. have strict rules and policies that limit you company's flexibility in how you market and sell your products.

When selling on Amazon, for example, you don't know who is buying your product. So you can't easily contact them or send follow-up messages. They're Amazon's customer, not yours.

When you sell through any intermediary, including a bricks and mortar retailer, they will take a chunk of your profit, which is why selling direct is more profitable.

If you have your own site, you can send prospects to it. That means you will be able to capture your customers' email address, have control over your brand image, and develop a personal relationship with customers.

Website builders such as Wix, GoDaddy and SquareSpace are also not ideal, for the same reason as having a presence only on Facebook. You're limited in what you can do on such sites, and you're dependent on them. They could close you down; and moving your content to another platform is difficult. Yet over half of the world's websites are hosted by these platforms, which makes them vulnerable.

WHY YOU NEED MORE WEBSITE CONTENT THAN YOU THINK

Having a lot of high-quality, relevant, and informative content on your website provides many benefits:

Improved search engine optimization (SEO): Having a lot of well-written, keyword-rich content will improve your website's visibility in search engine results pages, which means you'll attract more traffic to the site.

Increased credibility: Providing detailed and comprehensive information about your products, services and company values will establish the business as an authority and build trust with potential customers.

A better user experience: A website with a wealth of content will provide a more engaging and informative experience for visitors, encouraging them to spend more time on the site and explore more pages.

A better understanding of products and services: Having detailed information about your products and services helps customers better understand what you have to offer and make informed purchasing decisions.

Increased engagement: Offering a range of content, such as a blog, videos and infographics, will encourage visitors to engage with your website, share content, and return for more information in the future.

MOBILE-FIRST

Web designers love to show us images of a busy website, bustling with features. But the truth is, the majority of visitors see your site on their phone. What they see is a simplified version of your site.

This means you should avoid the expansive charms offered by the web designer, and demand to see what it looks like on a screen that measures just two and a half inches (6cm) wide.

How does your six-column table work on a phone? What does your feature comparison board look like?

Having mobile-centric look on your site ensures a positive user experience for the increasing number of mobile users.

It starts with you designing the site with mobile devices as the primary platform, ensuring that content and functionality is optimized for smaller screens, touch-based interaction and fast loading times.

Otherwise, you may face challenges such as low engagement and poor user experience for mobile visitors, leading to lower search engine rankings, and decreased conversions.

SEND USEFUL EMAILS

We've talked a lot about emails throughout this book, but now is the time to examine *why* they're so important, and *how* to use them to best advantage.

The one massive advantage of an email list is that you own and control it, which isn't true of your contracts on Facebook and Instagram.

It's a tireless worker, delivering content to your loyal fans while you sleep.

And when you send an email, you aren't fighting in a crowded space for their attention. You only have to see people flicking restlessly though Facebook to know how hard that is.

Your email list has two functions:

1. Build a tribe. You achieve that by giving them helpful advice and interesting information. As we've seen earlier, it's "give to get".

2. Increase sales, by occasionally sending them news about new products and special offers.

9 Ways to make your emails work harder

1. **Pay attention to your subject line**. If it looks spammy, they'll report you. And if it's dull, they won't open it. A three- to four-word subject line produces the best response.

2. **Don't limit yourself to three or four emails**. Few people

buy on the first contact. And it's not unknown for a prospect to make their first purchase five years after subscribing.

3. **Get the frequency right**. If you leave too long a gap, they'll forget who you are and unsubscribe. Do it too often and you'll irritate them. Depending on your market, consider sending an email weekly for the first month, then monthly thereafter.

4. **Segment your email list** into prospects and repeat buyers, or buyers of different products; and send appropriate messages to each.

5. **Create a sequence of evergreen pre-written emails**. This saves time. It works on the basis of 'Create once, then use forever'.

6. **Get the reader to click a link on the email** to your site. That way, they're more likely to buy. This means you don't need too much copy in your email.

7. **Ask questions**. It fosters engagement, which in turn creates sales.

8. **Test your subject line** and content to improve your results.

9. **Make 80% of your emails informative**, with only 20% being a sales message.

PROVIDE FAQS

There are those who dislike the traditional Frequently Asked Questions (FAQ) page. They say it's a dumping ground for company information, it's unstructured, and it's hard for visitors to understand. They say a well-designed website doesn't need it.

But even after all these years, the FAQ page still has a role to play. For many visitors, it's a go-to place they're familiar with. It solves people's problems, prevents negative reviews, and increases internal page views. It also boosts your search ranking.

Having a FAQ page on a website allows customers to quickly find answers to common questions about the business, its products, and services. This not only saves time for the customer, but also reduces the workload for the business' customer service team, who would otherwise need to handle repetitive inquiries. By providing customers with easy-to-find answers, businesses can build trust and demonstrate your expertise in your field.

In addition to a website, adding a FAQ section to printed marketing materials such as brochures, flyers, and business cards can also be beneficial. This allows customers to access information about the business even when they are offline, making it easier for them to make informed decisions about whether to use the business' products or services.

A software company could include a FAQ section on its website and in its product brochures to answer common questions about installation, compatibility and features. An e-commerce store should include a FAQ section on its website and in its shipping and return policy information to answer questions about shipping times, return procedures, and payment options.

How to create a great FAQ page

1. Understand the questions. Know what people need to find out. And recognise that visitors don't necessarily use the same words as you.

2. Categorize the questions. Structure them into logical sections, such as products, delivery, returns, your account and so on.

3. Have a search bar. It lets people get to the answer faster.

4. Keep the FAQ page updated. As time goes by, your products and people's needs change.

5. Bear in mind that a FAQ page should support a well-structured website, not be a substitute.

KEEP YOUR WEBSITE SIMPLE BUT INFORMATIVE

According to the Baymard Institute, 59% of sites use overly aggressive and distracting ads on the homepage.

Doing so can negatively impact sales for several reasons:

- **Worse user experience**: Distracting content and ads (including boxes promoting your own products) create a cluttered and confusing homepage, causing users to become frustrated and quickly leave the site, potentially leading to a higher bounce rate.

- **Decreased credibility**: An excessive number of in-house ads decrease the credibility and trust in your brand, leading users to seek alternatives.

- **Reduced engagement**: Distracting ads can pull the users' attention away from the actual products or services being offered on the site, potentially reducing engagement and interest in making a purchase.

So it is important to strike a balance between promoting products and services and providing a positive user experience. A clean, well-designed homepage with strategically placed, non-intrusive ads can be more effective in generating sales.

At the Gap website, the visitor gets deluged with a range of offers and a popup, which makes for complexity. It also has a search bar with moving text, and a countdown timer.

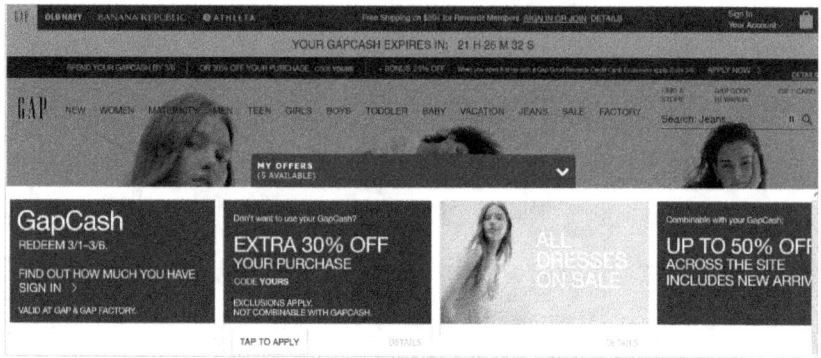

There are four distracting offers on the Gap website

Mass market e-tailers like to make their site look exciting, while upmarket stores want to look exclusive. But there is a balance to be drawn between being excessive minimalist and overly complex.

How to audit the effectiveness of your website

1. Bear in mind that a web designer isn't necessarily business focused. Designers like interesting layouts and the next big idea in web design.

2. Carry out research to what your customers are looking for, and how easy it is to find. Companies like Userbrain and Loop11 have panels of people who will carry out sample tasks on your website and you can watch a recording of what problems they encountered.

3. Carry out A/B testing to identify marginal but important

improvements.

4. Implement the necessary changes.

AVOID OVERLY COMPLEX PASSWORDS

Requiring customers to use overly complex passwords reduces sales because it leads to customer frustration, decreased customer satisfaction and decreased customer trust. 82% of businesses fail to achieve this, according to the Baymard Institute.

If you require a customer to create a password with a minimum length of 16 characters, including uppercase and lowercase letters, numbers and special characters, they will have difficulty remembering it.

Customers can usually deal with complex passwords when setting up their account, but then can't remember the password when they return, which leads to login failure. Since only one in five people in the USA use a password manager, that's not surprising.

And your password-reset email may fail or go to spam, which increases frustration. 19% of people who request a new password abandon their shopping basket.

Some businesses use a one-time sign-in link, known as a "magic link", that allow users to bypass usual password process, but these can also fail.

Another problem is if your website periodically requires customers to reset their passwords. The customer may choose to shop elsewhere.

Some experts recommend a minimum length of eight characters; and this will depend on the scale of the security risk. Installing a reCAPTCHA will reduce the level of fraud. So will asking customers to re-enter their details if they want to change their address or email address. Another solution is to add a two-factor authentication, by asking the customer to confirm an order by email or SMS.

Allowing a customer to checkout as a guest also removes the need for a password.

How to minimize friction caused by passwords

1. Allow guest checkout.

2. Allow people to use eight or more characters of their choosing.

3. Minimize fraud by secondary means such as Captcha and 2FA.

4. Require 2FA for change of email or physical address.

5. Encrypt all customer information.

6. Maintain a strong password policy for employees.

7. Conduct regular security audits.

MAKE IT PERSONAL

When you meet someone and you get a friendly response, you'll want to meet them again. Equally, if they seem disinterested in you, that relationship is doomed.

So why should it be different with customers, especially now that we have so many tools to personalize our online interactions?

Customers appreciate being recognized and understood. And they feel valued when you personalize your communication.

Personalizing *face-to-face* interactions are crucial. It's hardest in a busy store where customers have only a brief transaction. But a friendly face and a greeting go a long way to making the customer feel wanted.

In *business-to-client relationships*, personalization is even more important, something we discuss in the section on Customer Tactics.

But here we're talking specifically about digital issues.

You can personalize your online marketing communication by using your customer data. That includes their demographic information, purchase history, and their behavior on the website. It lets you create dynamic content that's customized to each customer's individual needs.

For e-commerce you can use your customer's purchasing record to recommend products that are similar to those they already bought. And a fashion retailer, say, can use demographic information to show the latest fashion trends for a specific age group or gender.

As you might expect, personalized emails get a better response than generic ones. Click through rates grow 14% and conversion rates are up 10%, according to Campaign Monitor.

By using your customer's name in the subject line and greeting, you create a more personal connection with your customer. You can use email to offer promotions and discounts based on your customer's purchase history or to share relevant news and product updates.

How to personalize your site

1. Search Google for 'marketing personalization' for suppliers and more ideas.

2. Decide what kind of personalization your customers or users would benefit from.

3. Include the actual name of the person you're communicating within the content you're sharing.

LAUNCH YOUR OWN APP

An app takes customers away from the hurly-burly world of competing brands and into a secure, calmer environment where they can get tailor made information, engage with you and order products.

The data is stored on the customer's phone, which means they get a faster response. The data is more personalized, and the customer gets better notifications. The phone may also give access to its functions such as the accelerometer, contact list and camera.

All this means you can provide a convenient and accessible platform for your customers to interact with you.

Industries that find mobile apps useful include:

Healthcare: for monitoring heart rate, improving mental health and aiding sleep.

Education: Interactive learning, individualized progress, testing and monitoring progress, immersive learning such as videos and podcasts.

Travel and Tourism: for bookings, notifications, and customer support.

Ecommerce: purchasing, rewards programs, tracking deliveries, and camera.

Finance: Reducing risk and fraud, updated bank balances, online transactions.

Walgreen's mobile app lets users refill prescriptions just by scanning a barcode. You can arrange a live video chat with an online doctor, set pill reminders, and check product availability in nearby stores.

The app is currently used by five million customers each month, and it has been downloaded 50 million times.

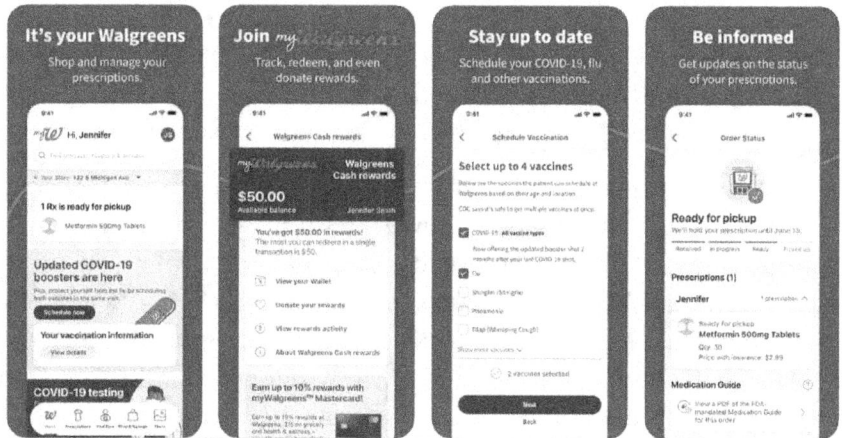

Walgreen's mobile app

How to create your own app

1. Decide whether your customers need an app. Identify what advantages it might give them.

2. Agree the app's functionality.

3. Select a suitable software contractor to create the app.

4. Carry out user experience testing.

5. Set the app to live.

CREATE A USEFUL TOOL

There are three types of useful online tools:

Internally-focused efficiency tools, such as Google Docs, Hootsuite or Asana. These needn't detain us here as they relate to staff efficiency. I mention them only for the sake of completeness.

Internally-focused marketing tools, such as CRM programs, Salesforce and Mailchimp. Where relevant I have commented on them in specific topics, notably Automate your marketing.

Customer-focused third-party marketing tools. These include software such as helpdesk, appointment booking and chat software. Check out Automate your marketing.

Customer-focused tailor-made tools. These are particularly interesting, because they solve customers' problems. Take temporary fencing. They're used on almost every construction site on the planet. But working out how many panels, connectors, feet and stabilizers you need is hard. And the price will depend on how you want, which usually requires you to email a request to the business. You can easily end up with too many or too few items which will add delay, frustration and cost. It would be better to have a tool that lets you input the length of fencing. It could then calculate the quantity of items you need, and give you a price.

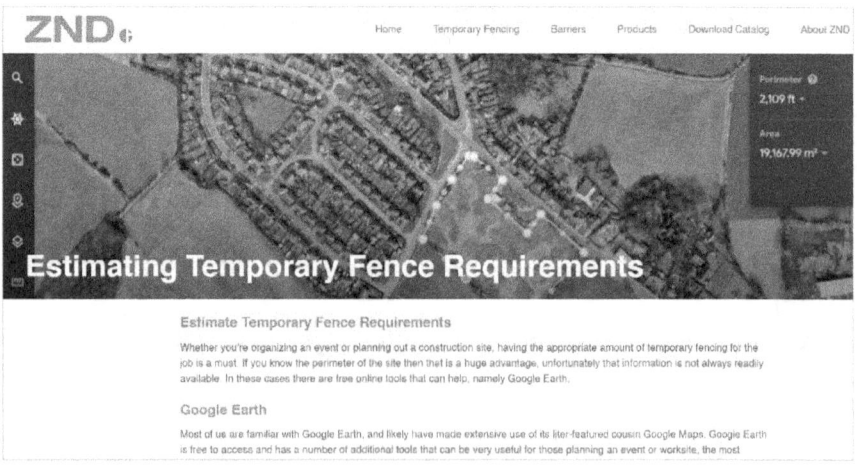

This website suggests you use Google Earth to calculate what length of fencing you need. It adds that you'll need to manually calculate all the accessories you'll need. Somehow, that doesn't seem easy.

An interactive tool on your website could solve customers' problems. It could be an analyzer, calculator, optimizer or a tester. By offering an interactive experience, you can create a more engaged and loyal customer base.

A fashion retailer could offer a virtual try-on tool that allows customers to see how an item of clothing would look on them. This provides an interactive shopping experience and reduces returns due to sizing or fit issues.

A financial services company can offer a retirement savings calculator that helps customers estimate how much they need to save to achieve their retirement goals.

How to create a useful tool

1. Review the process customers go through to buy your product. Do they have to make calculations, analyze data, visualize it, optimize a layout or cutting pattern, or compare options?

2. Define the data that customers input, and the outcome they want.

3. Include the options they might need, such as quantity, location or quality.

4. Decide how the information should be stored and delivered.

5. Hire a developer to create the tool.

6. Test and implement it.

A/B TESTING

Tiny gains matter. As James Clear notes in his book Atomic Habits:

if you can get 1 percent better each day for one year, you'll end up thirty-seven times better by the time you're done. Conversely, if you get 1 percent worse each day for one year, you'll decline nearly down to zero. What starts as a small win or a minor setback accumulates into something much more.

And that's the power of A/B testing. It's a method of comparing two versions of your product or service (version A and version B) to determine which one performs better.

You do this by dividing a sample of users into two groups, with each group receiving a different version of the product. You then analyze the results to see which version performed better in terms of conversion rate, click-through rate or engagement.

You might conduct an A/B test to determine the most effective page design. By testing two different versions of the page, you can find out which design is more likely to lead to a purchase.

Or you could conduct an A/B test to determine the best call-to-action (CTA) button color, text, and placement. By testing two different versions of the CTA, you can determine which version is more likely to lead to a download or purchase.

A/B testing is relevant for email marketing. You can conduct an A/B test to determine the best subject line, sender name, and email body for a promotional email. By testing two different versions of the email, you can ascertain which version is more likely to result in higher open rates, click-through rates, and conversions.

Let customers compare product features

Allowing customers to compare products and their features on your website has several benefits:

1. **Ease of decision making**: When customers can compare products side by side, they can easily see the differences in features and specifications, making it easier for them to make an informed decision on what product to purchase.

2. **Increased trust and credibility**: By providing customers with clear and transparent information about products, a company can increase the trust and credibility of its brand.

3. **Competitive advantage**: By offering a comparison feature, you can differentiate your business from competitors and stand out in a crowded market.

4. **Better customer experience**: Allowing customers to compare products can make the shopping experience easier and more enjoyable, potentially leading to increased customer satisfaction and loyalty.

All this assumes that you have a range of similar products or services. But even businesses with a limited product range often have options such as delivery or bundles. SaaS companies often benefit from a pricing table.

This Apple Watch comparison table provides an image and a brief overview of each, followed by detailed features and functionality.

How to implement a features table

1. Decide on the features you want to compare.

2. Set up the features in a spreadsheet or database.

3. Decide whether you want to include features such sorting and filtering.

4. Get a web designer to translate this on to your website.

GATED CONTENT AND DOWNLOADS

Content is good, but you don't necessarily to make it all public. Why? Because you might hold some back as an inducement to visitors. This applies particularly to B2B markets, where each visitor could become a lucrative client. And offering them a download, for which they must hand over their email address, is a good way to capture their details.

By requiring potential customers to provide contact information or fill out a form, you can build a database of leads who have shown interest in your products or services. You can then use this information for targeted marketing and sales efforts.

You could offer a white paper or an eBook, one that provides in-depth information on a topic related to your products or services. In exchange for access to this information, you require the visitor to fill out a form with their contact information. This allows you to follow up the lead, and nurture the relationship, ultimately leading to a sale.

You could also offer a free trial or demo of a product in exchange for contact information. By giving potential customers the opportunity to experience the product first-hand, you can build trust and demonstrate the value of your service. This can be especially effective for technology and software businesses.

You can segment and prioritize those leads by including questions about their industry, job title, the number of employees at their organisation, and their country.

How to create gated content

1. Identity the content that prospects would find most valuable.

2. Create the content, whether an eBook, course or white paper.

3. Set up a web page or side bar that promotes the content.

4. Create the download form.

5. Follow up with regular emails.

Show people and uses in your marketing

You're buying packing chips online, the kind of loose-fill you use to protect valuable items.

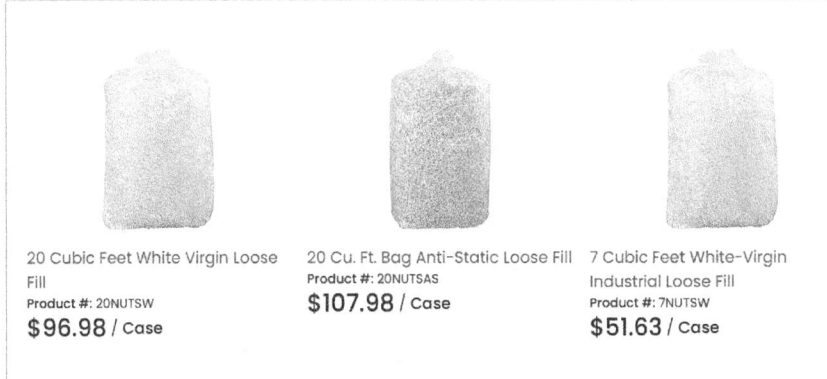

20 Cubic Feet White Virgin Loose Fill
Product #: 20NUTSW
$96.98 / Case

20 Cu. Ft. Bag Anti-Static Loose Fill
Product #: 20NUTSAS
$107.98 / Case

7 Cubic Feet White-Virgin Industrial Loose Fill
Product #: 7NUTSW
$51.63 / Case

But from the image above can you work out how big the bags are? It would have been more helpful if the company had shown them against a human.

Using real people in product advertisements and on the company website helps establish trust and credibility with potential customers. You may spot users' comments on Amazon saying they hadn't realized how small the camera/knife/vase was.

Seeing people using the product in a natural, relatable setting can help customers imagine themselves using the product and better understand its application. It can also create a more emotional connection to the product and make it feel more accessible and desirable.

Solely showing images of the product may come across as inauthentic or impersonal, making it more difficult for customers to connect with the product and the company.

GUEST CHECKOUT

Providing a guest checkout option leads to more sales because it reduces friction in the checkout process.

34% of people who abandoned their shopping cart said it was because they had to create an account. And since 70% of all carts are abandoned, that means you lose 24% of all your revenue if you don't have a guest checkout.

Creating an account is a time-consuming and tedious process. This is especially true for customers who are not familiar with the website or are making a one-time purchase. It's also especially true for customers buying on their mobile phone, because the form fields are small, and the phone doesn't have a mouse.

You should make the guest checkout prominent because it increases its visibility and makes it easier for customers to find. If the guest checkout option is not obvious, your customers may abandon their purchase or switch to a competitor's site.

You may need customers to have an account if you expect them to interact with your site. But you can email the customer later, and invite them to register.

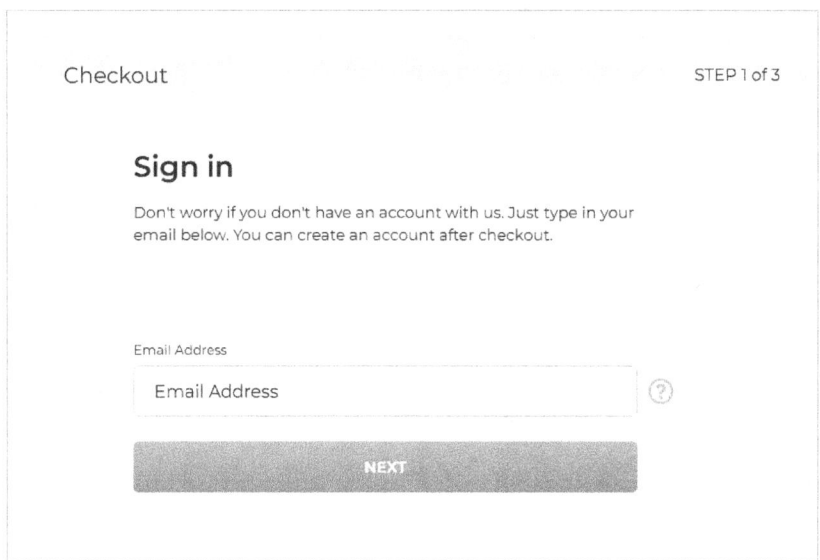

Checkout   STEP 1 of 3

Sign in

Don't worry if you don't have an account with us. Just type in your email below. You can create an account after checkout.

Email Address

| Email Address | ? |

NEXT

This fuels business makes it easy for customers to check out.

AUTOMATE THE ADDRESS COMPLETION

55% of websites don't automate their checkout address. This leads to errors and abandoned carts when shoppers make a mistake. This can include typing errors (which can lead to a failed delivery), not knowing a zip/postcode, or not understanding what to do about an error. As you might expect, shoppers experience increased problems with mobile devices.

Automated address completion

PROVIDE ONLINE CHAT

For the consumer there are many advantages of letting consumers communicate using online chat:

- **Fast**: Chat enables real-time communication and lets consumers to get their queries resolved quickly.

- **Convenient**: Chat allows customers to get quick answers to their questions or resolve issues without having to call or email. This can save time and effort for the customer.

- **Accessible**: Online chat is accessible to everyone, including individuals with disabilities who may have difficulty using the phone. Some companies (though not many) have a 24-hour service, which means people can contact you outside work hours. And if you operate globally, your 11pm may be their 10am.

- **Personalized**: Chat enables customers to have a real-time, personalized interaction with a company representative. This can lead to a more positive customer experience and help build trust and loyalty.

Overall, chat gives a more personal and interactive experience for consumers, leading to improved customer satisfaction. And for the company there are definite benefits:

- **Cost-effective**: Online chat is cost-effective for you as it requires fewer resources compared to telephone support. Agents can handle more than one call at a time. And chat tends to be faster than phone calls. Customers have to type a question, which focuses their mind. Al of this makes chat more efficient for you, and reduces waiting times.

- **Increased sales**: By providing prompt and efficient support, chat can help increase customer confidence and lead to increased sales. In addition, chat can be used proactively to offer recommendations and help guide customers towards making a purchase.

How to implement a chat system

1. Identify whether prospects and customers would benefit from a chat facility.

2. Decide whether you can staff a chat service, or outsource it.

3. Review the various chat programs, select one, and install it on your website

4. Set up agents and standard responses.

CREATE A COMMUNITY

Building a community takes time and effort, but it increases customer engagement, loyalty and advocacy.

There has to be a strong reason for members to join. What benefits will they get? How will you make it worth their time to engage with each other and with your brand?

And if you want it to grow, you must make it easy and valuable for members to encourage others to join.

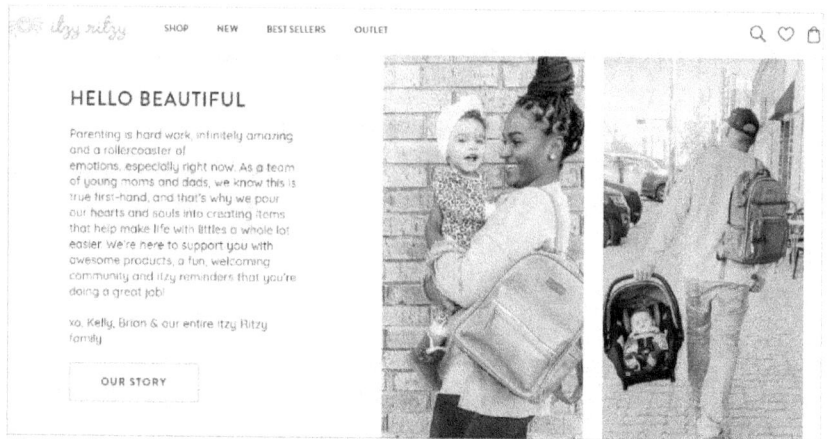

Itzy Ritzy has an active community, with a rewards program, consumer reviews and Instagram posts.

Note that a *community* is not the same as an *audience*. A community is 'many to many', whereas an audience is 'one to many'. You've got a community if, when you stop creating content, the talk keeps flowing. In other words, a community involves User Generated Content.

The best way to create a community is to set it up where people already are, such as Facebook or Reddit. It's harder to get people to make a special trip your website.

Here are some of the many ways to build a community:

- **Engage them with social media**: Have a closed group on Facebook or similar platform, to give people a greater sense of community. Use an open page to engage with customers, create and share relevant content, and respond to customer inquiries and feedback.

- **Encourage user-generated content**: Get customers to

share their experiences, feedback, and ideas through reviews, surveys, and forums.

- **Have a loyalty program**: Implement a loyalty program that rewards customers for their continued business and encourages them to be active members of the community.

- **Community-driven events**: Host events such as webinars, workshops, and meet-ups to bring customers together and foster a sense of community.

- **Influencer marketing**: Partner with influencers who use your product, to promote your brand and reach a wider audience.

- **Customer service**: Provide excellent customer service and make customers feel valued.

- **Personalize it**: Use data and customer insights to personalize your marketing and communication efforts.

- **Socially responsible values**. Consumers are drawn to organisations that offer more than just wanting their money. A genuine and consistent commitment to the environment, local needs or other values are important.

HAVE A HELPDESK

The phone keeps ringing with customer queries and problems. You manage to log most calls, and resolve many of them. But some get answered late, or not at all. Customers get irritated. Support staff are stressed and over-worked.

And that's why many businesses need a helpdesk. It's a way to corral and respond to customer problems. Zendesk, Help Scout, SysAid and Spiceworks are just some of the products available.

A help desk ensures that customers' questions are structured properly, so your staff get the right information. It speeds up their response, stops the back-and-forth, and gives users a more accurate answer.

You can also identify customers' patterns, and optimize your support processes, for example by using canned responses.

Customers can quickly find answers to their questions, get technical support, and even request a refund or return. This streamlined process improves the customer experience and reduces the need for customers to contact customer service agents.

An online helpdesk reduces customer support costs by automating routine tasks and providing self-service options. For example, Spotify has an online help center that provides customers with a range of resources, including FAQs, troubleshooting guides, and community forums. This reduces the burden on customer support agents and allows the company to provide support 24/7.

Lastly, an online helpdesk increases operational efficiency by providing insights into customer behavior and preferences. They provide a range of analytics and reporting tools. You can use this data to identify patterns, optimize your support process, and improve your overall customer experience.

Prior to instituting a Happy Fox helpdesk, the appliance manufacturer Whirlpool would take inbound emails from each of its 32 factory email inboxes, as well as from its financial accounts, and import the data into a spreadsheet for each.

After installing the help desk, Whirlpool was able to reduce incoming emails by 15-20%. But it also saw improvements in other areas. Its suppliers were no longer sending in multiple emails for the same query, and it let the company handle suppliers' accounts in a more proactive manner.

That's it!

We've covered a great many tactics in this book, both for digital and bricks-and-mortar activity.

Finally, on the next page, there are suggestions for additional steps you can take.

When in doubt, take the next step.
- Regina Brett

12. YOUR NEXT STEPS

1. Write a quick review. If this book helped you, give it a short review on Amazon, so other people can find it and benefit from it. Just a couple of lines is enough. Here's the link:

https://mybook.to/tactical-marketing

Or point the camera on your phone at the QR code.

Your review matters more than you know, because it will help others find the book.

If you leave a review, be sure to tell me at KitSadgrove@gmail.com

2. Email me about your marketing journey. Let me know if I've omitted a marketing tactic, so I can add it to the book. I read every email I get.

3. Buy a copy of my recent book: Copywriting Frameworks, Formulas and Checklists.

4. Get help to improve your marketing at ixant.com. I work with a limited number of clients each year to identify their route to increased sales and profit, using the 9 LeversTM tactical program.